BOOKS BY

Laurie Kanyer, MA

Collage Care: Transforming Emotions and Life Experiences with Collage

Twenty-Five Things to Do When Grandpa Passes Away, Mom and Dad Get Divorced or the Dog Dies: Helping Children Cope with Loss or Change

The Journey of Becoming a Mother: Tools for a New Mother's Emotional Growth and Development

Parent Connection: Building Attachments Between Parent and Child

Collage Care

Transforming Emotions and Life Experiences with Collage

Written by Laurie Kanyer, MA

Co-created by Sarah Best | Edited by Wyatt Kanyer
Content curated by Lillian Cassidy | Junior design by Jennifer Waldsmith
Cover art by Michael DeSutter | Senior design by JuSt Design

First Edition

Published by Kanyer Publishing
Yakima, Washington, USA

2021

Kacylia Pistoia, *Finding a Place of My Own*, 2019, Collage, Doug + Laurie Kanyer Art Collection

Praise for *Collage Care*

"Flowing through the pages of this book is the fabric of healing, threaded by Laurie's deep passion for collage and her rooted nature to be in service to others. Using her life's work, Laurie offers an accessible framework to guide readers through the therapeutic nature of this medium. *Collage Care* combines artistry with majesty through its commune of collage as a tool for transformation. Each Gem contextualizes its power and reveals a pathway towards our liberation. If you are seeking to create the life you deserve, this book is for you."
—Sheila Darcey, Artist and Author of *Sketch by Sketch - The Creative Path to Emotional Healing and Transformation*

"*Collage Care: Transforming Emotions and Life Experiences With Collage* is a significant contribution to the relatively sparse body of literature that focuses on the benefits of the collage-making process to emotional well-being. Laurie Kanyer provides an indispensable compendium of how collage promotes self-awareness, experimentation, and acceptance. This compelling guide offers a practical and accessible format for those interested in collage; artists looking to boost their creativity, art therapists, and their clients alike. I recommend this book wholeheartedly."
—Tanja Ulbrich, MA Social Sciences, Gestalt Art Therapist

"If you aren't including collage in your visual art curriculum, what are you waiting for? With over 125 Gems and examples of powerful contemporary collage, this book clearly demonstrates that creating through collage will be impactful for students beyond learning the basic elements of art and design. Kanyer shows us that students at all levels can approach collage and make artwork that is technically competent as well as insightful, communicative, and reflective."
—Dana Caldera, Artist and Art Professor

"The beautiful thing about collage is its accessibility to anyone with just a few tools. Laurie takes this creative process and turns it into a tool—in and of itself—to aid in communication, processing, and self expression. It offers beautiful examples, helpful prompts, and leads self exploration to enlightening results."
—Hollie Chastain, Collagist, Author of *If You Can Cut, You Can Collage: From Paper Scraps to Works of Art*

"This book describes 125 ways collage can help. I couldn't believe it at first, but all of these Gems are true! I recognize myself in the different ways collage transforms lives as outlined in Kanyer's book. *Collage Care* proved how a couple of simple tools, a pair of scissors and a glue stick can bring light in dark times. When I thought I had nothing, I had collage."
—Angela Gobbens, aka @miss.printed, founder of The Scandinavian Collage Museum, The Collage Club, and The Collage Garden, Co-founder of Februllage and the inventor of the Locative Collage

"*Collage Care: Transforming Emotions and Life Experiences with Collage* is a book about connections; the connections our brains make between our experiences, the connections that occur when creating collage, and the connections between collage and mental care. Much like the practice of collage itself, Laurie Kanyer layers a patchwork of Gems on the medium of collage to create an empowering tool that can help lead you on a journey of mental, emotional, and physical recovery. *Collage Care* is an accessible guide for both artists and non-artists alike, and provides readers with the skills they need to create lasting change."
—Matt McCarthy, Collagist

"Collage is God's way of uniting the universe."

—Skip Brea

This book is dedicated to:

Darwin Kanyer
My Father-in-law
January 17, 1925 - October 30, 2020

Darwin came to know about the magic of collage in his 95th year from numerous conversations we had while he was ill. He passed away while this book was being written.

&

Wesley Douglas Dahlhauser
My Grandson
October 11, 2017

May you know the wonders of art and especially collage!

&

Connie Dawson
September 15, 1934 - May 14, 2021

Connie had a significant role in every book I have written, including *Collage Care*. Connie was a constant mentor, teacher, encourager and guide, since 1994. As an author and therapist, she helped to free thousands from the chains of shame and emotional hardships.

Laurie Kanyer, *Somewhere Out There*, 2019, Collage, Doug + Laurie Kanyer Art Collection

"Collage is a curiosity in the most intense meaning of the word."

—Mario Zoots

Mario Zoots, *Egg*, 2018, Collage, Doug + Laurie Kanyer Art Collection

CONTENTS

Lee McKenna, *How Does Your Garden Grow II*, 2019, Collage, Doug + Laurie Kanyer Art Collection

ABOUT THE COLLECTOR'S EDITION

The Collector's Edition of *Collage Care* features over 150 full color images of fine art collage, created by 132 artists from the Doug + Laurie Kanyer Art Collection. *Collage Care* is essentially a private tour of that collection, which focuses exclusively on the acquisition of collages from the year 1980 to the present. The Kanyers are among very few private art collectors who are building a collection exclusively of collage. The Kanyer's mission is to collect collage solely for the purpose of magnifying the genre from a historical perspective, and to support and encourage collagists. The Collection has over 900 fine art collages, and the Collector's Edition of *Collage Care* showcases collagists worldwide. Most of the artists have been using collage as their primary art practice for decades. It is the intent of the collectors to donate the Collection to a worthy institution.

This Collector's Edition is a fine art book AND a healing tool offering transformation of emotional well-being. *Collage Care* the Collector's Edition features 125 Gems of empirical evidence, discovered by Laurie Kanyer in her practice as a counselor. The book documents how using collage is transformative.

The Collector's Edition is also a fine art coffee table book and a record of the importance of collage from a psychological perspective. Kanyer knows from her work as a counselor the powerful psychological benefits of viewing art—be it the art on a record cover, a professional photo of a sports hero in a magazine, a painting by one of the old masters, or fine art collages—like those featured here. Including fine art collages in this volume, with an emphasis on emotional well-being, is intended to enhance the reader's transformation and healing. Art inspires and defines our lives beyond the walls of a museum.

Doug and Laurie Kanyer, who live in the high desert region of Central Washington, USA, began collecting art in 1978 as college students. The Kanyers have been compared to Herb and Dorothy Vogel, acquiring art on a shoestring. Similar to the Vogels, in their early days of collecting the Kanyers would make small monthly installments to the artists they collected. Married in 1981, they have collected art throughout their lives together. Artists residing in the Central Washington area were the initial focus of their collecting efforts. The original intent of the Collection was to donate the entire Collection to the Yakima Valley Museum, as a historical record. In 2017 they donated the bulk of the Central Washington arm of the Collection—including a majority of works they inherited from artist Charles A. Smith—to the Museum in honor of the retiring director, John Baule. The donation, of over 200 large and small scale works, was the largest acquisition of art in the history of the museum.

Laurie Kanyer, who is an artist herself, used collage as a healing tool with her students and clients dating back to 1986. In 2016 she began to incorporate collage into her own art practice in an effort to calm her spirits in the face of a family medical crisis. Some 350 collages later, she knew the value of collage on a personal level, too. This led the couple to begin to collect collage, in addition to art by Central Washington artists.

In 2019, at the encouragement of *Kolaj Magazine* Publisher Ric Kasini Kadour, they decided to dedicate all future collecting efforts solely to collage. "Collectors sustain their intention over a period of time. They use the objects they collect to further and deepen their understanding. Collectors build a story, piece by piece, with each item they add," said Kadour (Kadour, 2019). The Kanyers, as noted by collagist Clive Knights, are interested in the human condition—using the vehicle of art to enhance the well-being of people and raise their spirits. The Kanyers know that art opens a door to what it means to live well and to define one's culture—to show with an image one's desired composition for a quality life (Knights, 2020).

With the publication of *Collage Care* Collector's Edition, the Kanyers are offering an opportunity for readers to enjoy a private showing of the Doug + Laurie Kanyer Art Collection and to learn ways to improve emotional well-being. Seeing and making art improves the quality of the lives of humans! Please visit the Collection website at www.kanyerartcollection.com and follow on Instagram (@kanyerartcollection) to see more.

FEATURED ARTISTS

From the Doug + Laurie Kanyer Art Collection

Aaron Beebe - USA
Adam Lalonde - USA
Alexandria Valentine - USA
Allan Bealy - USA
Andrea Burgay - USA
Anne Misfeldt - Denmark
Antonio Guerra Álvarez - Spain
Axelle Kieffer - France - USA
Ben DiNino - USA
Betty Klaasse - The Netherlands
Bill Noir - France
Bonnie Denver Ruttan - USA
Brian Barker - USA
Camila Fernández - Argentina
Carlotta Speroni - Italy
Carol White - Ireland - USA
Cecil Touchon - USA
Celia Crane - USA
Charles Wilkin - USA
Claire Standish - USA
Clare Celeste Börsch - Germany - USA
Clive Knights - USA - England
CP Harrison - USA
Dana Caldera - USA
Danielle Cole - Canada
Danielle Krysa aka The Jealous Curator -Canada
David Crunelle - Belgium
Della Wells - USA
Dennis Busch - Germany
Donna Morello - USA
Dorothée Mesander - Greece - The Netherlands
Emily Marbach - USA - England
Emma Anna - Australia - Colombia
Erin Houghtaling - USA
Fernanda Porto - Brazil - Germany
Frances Ryan - Scotland
Fred Free - USA
Gherdai Hassell - Bermuda - England
Henry Payer (Ho Chunk) - Winnebago Tribe of Nebraska - USA
Hollie Chastain - USA
HollyAnna DeCoteau Littlebull - (Wanahetite) Yakama Tribe of Washington - USA
Idris Veitch - Jamaica
Irie Wata - The Netherlands
Isabelle Milkoff - France - USA
Jake Kennedy - United Kingdom
James Gallagher - USA
Jane Chipp - United Kingdom
Janice McDonald - USA
Jasmine Romero - USA
Jay Berrones - USA - Mexico
Jennifer Sampson - USA
Jeremiah Duncan - USA
Jesse Freeman - USA
Jessica Whittingham – The Bahamas
Jim Ford - USA
John Gall - USA
John Whitlock - USA
Julia Payne - Canada - USA
Julie Liger-Belair - Canada
Juliette Pestel - The Netherlands
Kacylia Pistoia - France
Karen Coull - Australia
Kathy Starr - USA
Katie Blake - USA
Katie McCann - USA
Kayla Lamotte - USA
Kellette Elliott - USA
Kelly Schaub - USA
Kerith Lisi - USA
Kevin Geronimo Brandtner - Austria
Kevin Sampsell - USA
Kiki Buccini - USA
Lane - Greece
Lara Rouse - USA
Laura Weiler - USA
Laurence Briat - France
Laurie Kanyer - USA
Lee McKenna - Australia
Lisa Myers Bulmash - USA
Lisa Sheets - USA
Liza Petridou - Cyprus
Luciana Frigerio - USA
Madonna Mayfield - USA
Margarita Vera - Spain
Margot De Korte - The Netherlands
Mario Zoots - USA
Mark Watkins - England
Martina Pozzi - Spain
Matt McCarthy - USA
Máximo Tuja aka Max-o-matic - Spain
Meikel Church - USA
Michael DeSutter - USA
Miguel Ontiveros USA
Miloo (Emily Geirnaert) - France
Miranda Milward - United Kingdom
Miss Printed - Norway
Monique Vettraino - Canada
Morgan Bukovec - USA
Nancy Kay Turner - USA
Nick Baccari aka Mr. Babies - USA
Niko Vartiainen - Finland
Nina Fraser - Portugal
ØjeRum - Denmark
Oliver Lunn - United Kingdom
Peter Dowker - Canada
Petra Zehner - France
Rebeka Elizegi - Spain
Rhed Fawell - Scotland
Ricardo Miguel Hernández - Cuba
Roberta Guarna - Italy
Rocío Romero - Spain
Rosie Schinners - Canada
Sabine Remy - Germany
Sara Vattano - Italy
Sarah Best - USA
Sarah Cowling - Canada
Sarah Jarrett - United Kingdom
Scott Neff - USA
Stephen Payne - USA
Steven Rudin - USA
Susan Lerner - USA
Susanna Lakner - Germany
Teresa "Tess" Ettel - USA
Teri Fridley - USA
Terry Ringler aka Trash Riot - USA
Todd Bartel - USA
Twiggy Boyer - USA
Wyatt Kanyer - USA
Yannick Lowery - USA
Zach Collins - USA
Zoë Charlton - USA

PROLOGUE

by Clive Knights, BA, DipArch, MPhil
Collagist, Professor of Architecture

The process of coming to an understanding of oneself is much like the enduring relation between a host and a guest. There is a part of me that never succumbs to explicit rendition or clear account, a perpetual internal strangeness of sorts that another, more familiar part of me welcomes into conversation, hoping for reconciliation as they cohabit within a single, embodied psyche. Always already underway, therefore never a blank slate, my identity must be refigured over and over in the dynamic play of this back and forth between welcoming host and welcomed stranger. The traditional role of art practice, or poiesis, as Aristotle reminds us, is to seek out similarities in things that differ and to attempt to make them appear, to incarnate and make visible this tension between the familiar and the unfamiliar, in the work of art. The skill of the artist, and thus the efficacy of the art work, lay in not letting one cancel out the other, but in sustaining the fluctuation of our perception, as a viewer of such work, "in-between," resisting the safe harbor of settled concepts, conventional thought, or the univocal. Collage may well be the archetype of this endeavor, built from the spontaneous creative eruption of new relationships and connections amongst disparate, diverse, yet already prevailing images. Each collage is a manifestation of a new exchange between existing characters, each character always more than the fragment that bodies them forth, yet each never enough until enriched by the figurations they form with others, a visual interlocution, a mutual meeting of strangers, a togetherness, a oneness perhaps not attainable in quite the same way by any other means.

It so happens that we live in fragmentary times as the narratives of traditional symbols of unity fade, and we find ourselves amid an onslaught of disparate agendas each competing for our attention. In a culture that has proliferated the visual image like none before, it is both ironic and salutary that the act of collage-making might now shift to the foreground as a means of tending to our well-being. In mining new and profound meanings from the preponderance of the superficial, in cutting deep into the surface of ephemeral media, and in eliciting vital, new figurations from the shed skins of mass-communication, collage triumphs in this world like never before. A testament to the revelatory potential of understanding oneself by finding connectivity in a dismembered world, collage is a gymnasium for the imagination, a tour de force of limbering and stretching, intensifying and releasing. As such, collage promises to reorient its maker before new horizons of hope and belonging.

Clive Knights, *The Houseplant's Promise to the Captive*, 2020, Collage, Doug + Laurie Kanyer Art Collection

FOREWORD

by Andrea Burgay, Artist & Art Educator

When I was anticipating my first phone conversation with Laurie Kanyer, I wasn't sure what to expect. I knew that she had recently started the Doug + Laurie Kanyer Art Collection, a survey of collage art that includes many artists who I greatly admire. I knew that in partnership with ***Kolaj Magazine*** she had produced Kolaj Fest, an amazing event I'd attended the previous year where I met collage artists from all over the world. It's also where I launched my collaborative magazine ***Cut Me Up***. And from some of the artists who had already met Laurie, I heard that she was warm and very supportive, something you don't always hear about people on the business side of the art world.

I assumed that our phone call would be largely formal—that we'd talk about logistics and I'd share some of the concepts behind the piece that she had recently purchased for her collection. But it went much deeper very quickly. I think our first conversation was an hour and a half. Laurie was interested and excited to talk about my work. She quickly asked questions that got to the heart of things—where my work stems from and why I work with collage.

Collage has always been a way for me to create order from chaos, to sort and organize fragments of materials and create cohesion. It is a safe place to play out destructive urges and work with anger and aggression, using these energies to communicate about experiences. These methods have helped me cope with many traumas and painful events in my history.

Laurie understood these motives and related them in both her own practice working with collage and her experiences using collage in her counseling and education practice. She also shared what she'd learned through talking to the collage artists in her collection about how they came to work in this art form. She found that many of them have had painful life events or histories of hardships and trauma. Collage gave them a path to work through their life struggles.

Much of this was revelatory, but what she next described is what truly struck me. She described very specifically how and why collage helps. She articulated psychological effects of collage, many of which I related to—developing a sense of control, reframing situations to create new meanings and illustrating events of loss or disaster to establish deeper acceptance of these events. She described how methods of sorting and organizing materials mirror therapeutic processes of assembling fragments of memories to create a unified story or narrative. She also described the physiological healing properties of collage-making—the pacing of stress hormones that takes place through repetitive small motions, such as cutting or tearing.

This is the moment when I told Laurie that she needed to write these things down. This was important. Her background of 35 years as a therapist and her experience as a collage artist and collector gave her the multiple perspectives needed to make these insights. She was able to articulate all the ways that artists instinctively heal themselves that we don't always have awareness of or the language to convey. As artists, we do not always know the ways that our artistic processes help us. We may struggle to access these methods when needed. Beyond the scope of what we already know, there are many other ways that collage can help us to be explored. And, of course, there are many people who have no idea that collage has this incredible potential to help them cope with many problems. They simply need an invitation.

What Laurie has done is create a guide. She has laid out the ways in which collage can help with emotions and life experiences. She has written these 'Gems' of truth, which I encouraged her to document. They are designed to be highly-accessible, not just to artists, but to anyone interested in exploring themselves and their life through collage-making.

You can take the information in this book and begin to make collage artworks that have personal meaning and develop your own artistic language to communicate and share your story. The psychological results will be an overall deeper understanding of one's own life, leading to the ability to make choices based on this knowledge and to access healing.

Beyond the personal benefits, understanding all the ways that collage, or art in general, can help allows us to be custodians of this knowledge for others. As an arts educator in New York City public schools, I see over and over again the many ways that art benefits my students. The more we know about all the ways that art can help, the more tools we have to bring to others who need them.

This book offers a way to untangle how we're feeling about what is happening. We can use this information to identify our feelings, illustrate pain, decrease feelings of helplessness, and create a sense of control when we feel we have none. And the simplest of principles—finding humor, creating beauty, and increasing relaxation may be just what we need.

Take one of the Gems that calls to you and start making collage.

Andrea Burgay, *Reconstruction Physics*, 2019, Collage with Embroidery, Doug + Laurie Kanyer Art Collection

PREFACE

I came to use collage as a child making scrapbooks. Much like the Victorians before me, I was documenting my life and making art too. In doing so, I was able to express myself about the events of my life that were filled with hardships at every turn. The scrapbook became a diary of sorts, an effective way to tell about my experiences in a confidential manner. Ever since those early years, collage has had a continuous, healing presence, playing a profound role over the course of my life.

In 1986, while on staff at our community college, my department chair asked if I would be willing to teach a high school course in child psychology. It happened to be at the high school I had graduated from and I jumped at the chance. Little did I know, there was no textbook or curriculum and class was to begin in five days. With no time to spare, I formed a syllabus and gathered all the magazines I could find so the students could make collages on the topics I planned to teach. Making collages helped many of these students, some who were facing serious hardships, to share their stories with me and in turn, process their pain. Some years later, I learned many of those students would become therapists, doctors, school principals, and parents.

While working as an educator and counselor throughout the late 1980s, I used collage to help my clients. Frequently, I selected parenting magazines for the source material as the basis for their collages. Making collages helped them to consider their challenges. This was the advent of an abundance of materials on child rearing. Most of the resources, including my first book, *The Journey of Becoming a Mother: Tools for A New Mothers Emotional Growth and Development*, published in 1996, were written to help caregivers navigate parenting challenges. Using this material, I incorporated collage as a teaching aid—once again, tales of emotional stress and upset in relationships emerged from their collages. Just as with my high school students, after making collages, these women felt better and their connections with their children improved. Their new awareness extended into their daily lives.

As my interest to delve deeper into the world of collage grew, so did a desire to collect this remarkable art form. In 2019, for our 37th wedding anniversary, I gave my husband Doug the gift of collage for the rest of our lives. Doug and I began collecting art together in 1978 and we decided we would continue, focusing exclusively on collage. This was meant not only as a celebration of our love and friendship, but also as a mission to advance the medium.

There are very few private collectors of collage in the world, and we wanted to fill the void. This led to the Doug + Laurie Kanyer Art Collection, which, at present, includes over 900 collages from all over the world. This is not an investment collection, as all of these works will be donated to a worthy institution at some point in the future. The aim of the Collection is to show collage to be not just a process, but also a relevant and impactful medium of its own. We support artists by purchasing and commissioning works, while creating a comprehensive historical record of contemporary collage.

While the Collection has grown, so too has my relationship with the artists and the world of collage as a whole. In 2018, Doug and I helped sponsor Kolaj Fest, a collage symposium directed and hosted by *Kolaj Magazine*. After connecting with the publisher of *Kolaj* about my experience in using collage as a therapeutic agent, he asked if I would write more on the topic for his magazine. This resulted in the

Fernanda Porto, Aura, 2020, 3-D Mini Collages, Doug + Lau1rie Kanyer Art Collection

Ricardo Miguel Hernández, *El Diluvio / The Flood*, 2020, Collage with Found Photos, Doug + Laurie Kanyer Art Collection

publication of two articles, "Collage Saves: The Brain Chemistry of Collage" (Kanyer, 2018) and "Small Muscles and Something to Anchor Me" (Kanyer 2017). Theses articles set the groundwork for this book. Over time, I learned these articles resonated with other collage artists. Many shared with me the ways collage helped them to literally remain glued together as they navigated experiences of pain and suffering.

Two artists, Todd Bartel and Andrea Burgay, encouraged me to write a book and elaborate on what I knew. Having written books before, I was extremely hesitant. Writing a book is a difficult task, especially if you have dyslexia, as I do. I was overwhelmed by the idea, but Andrea suggested I begin by making a list of all the ways I knew collage could help. Within a day, I had 55 ways I knew collage helped. Soon after, another 65 found their way onto the page. The floodgate was open and 35 years of research on collage, emotions, and processing life experiences poured from my brain.

By April 2020, I was ready and eager to begin writing the book. It was the middle of the Coronavirus pandemic and I felt an urgency to get the information out into the world. The book you hold in your hands documents the empirical evidence, acquired both professionally and personally, of how the use of collage is a phenomenal tool for healing. I designed it to be accessible for all and to speak to a number of audiences.

If you are a seeker, looking to decrease the emotional weight of your life, you will find guidance and relief here. This book is not about how to become a master collage artist. It is about how making collages will support your well-being. This book will clearly explain for you how making collage will ease your discomfort. If you are a collagist, whether you create professionally or as a hobby, this book will tell you how making collages for your own well-being is a wise notion. It will reinforce the importance of making collage for yourself, first and foremost, while fortifying your practice as an artist and reminding you of the value of both.

This book is for therapists, teachers, youth workers, chemical dependency providers, those who work with the elderly or medically fragile—anyone in the helping professions can employ collage as one of their primary modalities to help people. This book outlines, for the first time, all the knowledge, insight and empirical evidence I discovered over 35 years on how using collage can transform emotions and life experiences. This material will help you in the work you do to help others.

This book is particularly significant for art historians. It marks an epoch in the historical timeline of the medium during a moment of increasing public interest and value. According to author Anila Babla (Putting the Pieces Together: Collage as a Mode in the Treatment of Trauma, Collage Research Network May 2020), there are four distinct historical phases of collage (to-date) and in the last several decades we have been in the "Reclaiming Identity" phase (Babla, 2020). People began this phase using collage to express sentiments of social movements, such as feminism, and to comment on race and identity. My professional work and the books I have written parallel these historical advocacy movements.

This collection of Gems—the 125 separate ways documented in this book proving how collage helps to transform emotions and life experiences—are historical evidence of the use of collage on a personal level; mining the issues of gender, memory, communication, race, identity (self-awareness), and problem solving. This book is a historical record, as it is the first time demonstrating how collage specifically, rather than other art medium, was used as a helping tool during this current historical phase.

What I can say for sure—as a person, an artist, and a professional—is that collage helped me and those I served. As an art collector interested in art history, I can say the fact that artists are using collage as a response to hardships offers insight into the art form's power and potency.

Laurie Kanyer, Central Washington, 2021

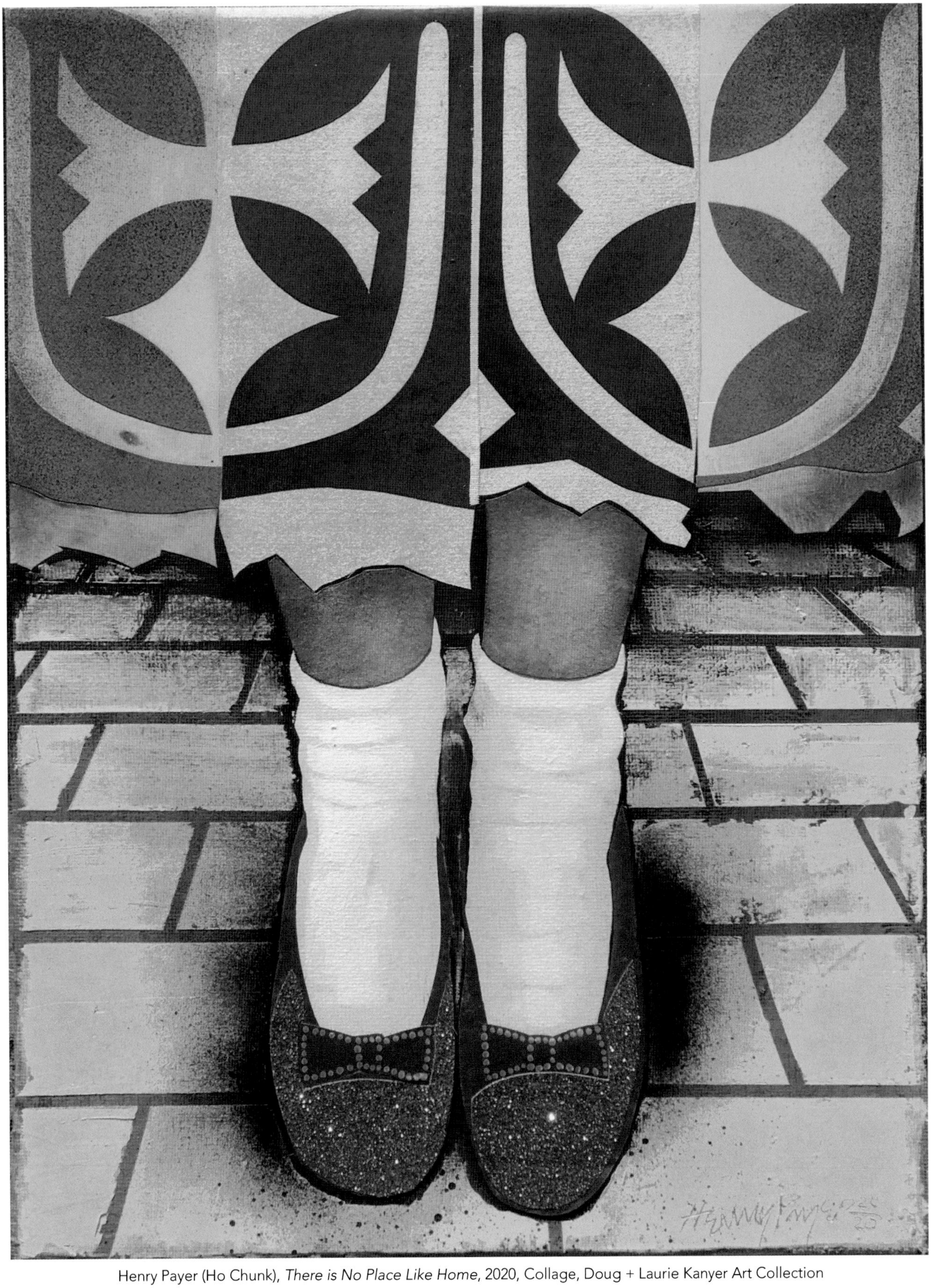

Henry Payer (Ho Chunk), *There is No Place Like Home*, 2020, Collage, Doug + Laurie Kanyer Art Collection

Mr. Babies, *Sunflower*, 2018, Collage, Doug + Laurie Kanyer Art Collection

Key Information

"We are a collage of our interests, our influences, our inspirations, all the fragmentary impressions we've collected by being alive and awake to the world. Who we "are" is simply a finely curated catalogue of those."

—Maria Popova

A BRIEF INTRODUCTION TO HOW COLLAGE TRANSFORMS

WELCOME, WE ARE GLAD YOU ARE HERE!

The book you are holding is the result of 35 years of comprehensive research into the benefits of collage on emotional well-being. Based on empirical evidence I collected as an educator, counselor, and artist, it includes 125 findings which demonstrate the expansive wonders of collage relative to easing emotions and examining life experiences. I refer to these findings as 'Gems' because they reflect precious truths that can immediately be put to work to improve the quality of your life. It is my hope that *Collage Care: Transforming Your Emotions and Life Experiences with Collage* will offer you vital support as you face the complexities and celebrations of life.

GEMS OF TRUTH ABOUT HOW COLLAGE TRANSFORMS

Within these pages, you will find over 125 powerful Gems of truth and ideas on the remarkable support you will experience in making collage. This book is a collection of ways collage helps to pace your emotions, solve problems, cope with potent social situations, make decisions, consider memories of the past, improve communication skills, evaluate life events, and improve relationships!

COLLAGE IS SIMPLE, BUT COMPLEX

Collage is a convenient and simple method you can quickly implement to address complicated life concerns. It is remarkable how the seemingly simple act of flipping pages, cutting paper, and gluing elements down can have a profound impact on your life.

COLLAGE MIRRORS LIFE

Often you reflect and ponder the events and experiences of your day. You are mentally gluing events, conversations, and related feelings together to form a visual mental construct. Like memories, the visual constructs that will make up a collage are stored in your mind and collectively reflect your lifetime. Collage helps you visually consider life, affirm your experiences, and offer reflections on your conclusions about what you experience. When completed, you can begin to process these memories not only emotionally, but physically. In this way collage mirrors the processes of life!

COLLAGE SOOTHES IN UNCERTAIN TIMES

During uncertain times of strain and hardship affecting the entire world—the pandemic of 2020, the AIDS epidemic, and the many World Wars come to mind—we need ways to soothe our emotions and frame the experiences connected to the unpredictability. When the entire world is facing hardship, the energy of the strain surrounds people like a thick fog. We know there is blue sky above the fog, but there is a hidden unknown as to when that fog will clear. This is heavy and burdensome on our emotions. The struggle we endure when faced with not being able to see the end to the confusion right in front of us causes undue suffering. We need ways to soothe the stress and isolation when a worldwide crisis comes upon us. Additionally, the ongoing tensions of life's daily pressures continue. The weight of what the world is facing is added to the burden of all other responsibilities. Collage will help to soothe you in times like these.

The word collage originates from the Greek word *kolla*. It then developed into the Old French *coller*, meaning to glue and this is what you could use right now. You need something to help you be more grounded or glued together at this tender time and for all of your life. Collage can do just that. It is the perfect tool to help you manage all the changes and daily strains.

Liza Petridou, *Finding Calm While We Wait: Life is Full of Colours*, 2020,
Digital Collage with Hand Painted Analogue Materials and Photograph, Doug + Laurie Kanyer Art Collection

COLLAGE CAN HELP YOU FEEL BETTER

Throughout my 35-year career as an educator and counselor, I have used collage with individuals and in groups, witnessing the improvement in the lives of those I served. I discovered that people could solve problems and make decisions using collage—helping them to move forward in their lives with more clarity and understanding. I witnessed their self-esteem and well-being improve, and came to understand collage as a powerful and transformative method by which to move through life.

This is not art therapy. I'm merely suggesting you can take care of yourself through the practice of collage. Just as eating healthy foods, exercising and getting plenty of sleep are fundamental in maintaining and improving your life quality, having a way to consider emotions and life struggles is important to your overall health, also. I intend to inspire you to add collage to your regular self-care routine. It will help decipher your feelings, provide ways to consider life concerns, and celebrate your joys and victories. As you use this book, you will come to know collage as your wonderful friend—readily available, loyal, honest, and true.

COLLAGE IS AFFIRMING

You do not have to be an artist or have artistic skills to make collages. Likely, you will be able to teach yourself how to do it through basic observation. The very nature of collage allows you to view it and immediately see ways to make collages yourself. Seeing is believing and it can be extremely motivating. By the simple (and enjoyable!) act of viewing the collages in this book, you will understand what to do and be motivated to make your own collages.

COLLAGE MEETS HUMAN NEEDS

Beyond the basics of food and shelter, people need to have predictability, security, and certainty in order to thrive. People need stimulating experiences and new learning opportunities. Connection, belonging, and acceptance with others is also key. You strive to remain flexible to daily changes while discovering ways to increase feelings of balance and predictability. You work to integrate and organize new information while finding a balance between too much stimulation and not enough. You search for ways to be part of something important with others, working to have meaningful connections to a group, while still maintaining your individuality.

When you are making a collage, you practice meeting central human needs. As you gather materials, search for the pleasing elements, shift the placement, and eventually glue them down; it is as if you are processing and providing for your needs. Collage echoes your journey to fulfill lifes needs and instills a sense of peace, comfort, and well-being.

COLLAGE OFFERS NEW INSIGHTS

In making collage, you are going to have new insights about yourself. You will understand others better and show yourself that you can be malleable, as you strive to gain peace and belonging. Collage gives you a way to create meaning and understanding of your life experiences, helping you feel more grounded. In viewing your finished collage (and maybe showing it to others) you will gain recognition, acceptance, and a sense of accomplishment. This will enhance your feelings of belonging and overall self-esteem, too. Additionally, when you are involved in creating, you are witnessing yourself as you make your collage. Collage affirms your very existence and further strengthens your sense of self and purpose in the world.

COLLAGE OFFERS AN IMAGE TO GAIN UNDERSTANDING

Collaging will offer you a chance to visually ponder your feelings and thoughts. It will help you to examine your conclusions and consider your choices. Collage helps you to modulate, regulate, and resolve your emotional response. This is one of the truly extraordinary and profound gifts of making a collage. It creates a tactual and visual image, helping you to acknowledge and accept the feelings and employ them as helpers in problem-solving. It will help you understand yourself better once the collage is complete. You can run your hands and fingers over the finished surface and literally feel your feelings—adding deeper affirmation and understanding.

Lisa Sheets, *Her Choices*, 2018, Collage on Board, Doug + Laurie Kanyer Art Collection

THIS BOOK IS FOR EVERYONE

Collage Care is for everyone who seeks an accessible way to transform emotions and life experiences. It is for seasoned artists and novices alike.The aim is not in making a masterpiece; you are merely making collages as a way to feel better. The goal is to learn about the profound value of collage and what a remarkable tool it is for improving your feelings, relationships, and overall well-being. You can use this book by yourself or with others.

SEEKERS

If you picked this book up because you're seeking guidance in handling hardships and are new to collage, you have come to the right place! You will gain insight as to how collage can be part of your life today. Reading the material while gazing upon the wondrous collages will inspire and support you in your exploration.

PROFESSIONAL ARTISTS

This book is very much intended for professional artists and collagists already versed in creating fine art. Whether using analog, digital, or mixed media methods, this book will validate why collage is valuable for you beyond your art practice. You will be surprised and delighted to learn of all the marvelous ways collage has supported your art practice and well-being. You will discover why a daily ritual of creating a collage is so vital on a deeper level.

HELPING PROFESSIONALS

This book is also for those in the helping professions. Whether you are a teacher, counselor, or work in other fields you can use this book to support those in your care. Collage is easily used one-on-one or in a group setting as a tool to help those you serve deal with their life concerns.

ART HISTORIANS AND SCHOLARS

This may be one of the first publications to show how collage is not only an important art form, but also a tool to help people cope with emotions and life experiences. This is incredibly relevant to art historians and those interested in art history. Collage is both a visual art form and a psychological coping mechanism, making it of historical importance.

Laura Weiler, *Yellow*, 2020, Collage, Doug + Laurie Kanyer Art Collection

GETTING TO KNOW THE LAYOUT OF THIS BOOK

Francis Bacon said this about books: "Some books are to be tasted, others to be swallowed, and some few to be chewed and digested; that is, some books are to be read only in parts; others to be read, but not curiously; and some few are to be read wholly, and with diligence and attention" (Armor, 1981). This book fits all of those descriptions.

A MULTITUDE OF CHOICES TO FIT YOUR NEEDS–THINK, CHOOSE, AND USE

In some ways, this book is like a collage itself. You can read it in a random fashion that suits you and what you are going through; or you can read it in an organized, sequential progression. You can read this book from front to back, or you can choose to jump around. It is like a toolbox where you see what you need to transform a project and you select what works for you. Like a restaurant menu, one day you may sample a Gem and implement the ideas immediately. Another day, you may read a Reflection to see how collage helped other people. Still later, you might study an Essay to gain more insight on collage. This book is to be used in a way that fits best for you.

GEMS

You will find 125 Gems of truth, the evidence I discovered on how collage supports the transformation of emotions and life experiences. The Gems are divided into topical sections and it is my hope you will read the Gems and use them as inspiration to make collages on your life experiences and the surrounding emotions you are experiencing.

WRITE OR COLLAGE YOUR OWN PERSONAL INSIGHTS

The margins are extra-wide on the Gems pages so you have room to make notes and chart your personal insights. Consider even adding some collage elements to the pages or make a complete collage inside the book, too!

REFLECTIONS–REAL LIFE TESTIMONIES

If you would like to read how using collage has transformed others' lives, turn to the end of the book where you will find reflective testimonies. The testimonies are from real people who experienced the power of collage during times of joy and hardships. They are written in each person's voice and demonstrate the wide variety of people who have transformed their lives with collage. Reflections are preserved in the voice and sentiment of the writer. Little if any editing was done so you could feel the impact of the transformational experience for each person.

ESSAYS

Are you a professional specializing in helping people or an art historian/scholar? At the back of the book you will find essays from several experts who describe why this material is essential in your field. The aim is to encourage you to use collage with those you serve to help them with their life circumstances. I invited these experts to write papers that speak directly to your profession in order to encourage further study of collage from an art history perspective and to verify the importance of the value of the Gems.

CP Harrison, *She Loves the Sounds of Sirens*, 2019, Collage, Doug + Laurie Kanyer Art Collection

A MEDITATIVE TOOL FOR TRANSFORMATION

You might consider using *Collage Care* for your daily meditation. Read a bit and then reflect on the information as part of your spiritual practice. Ponder the material, take what fits for you and leave ideas that don't seem to fit right now.

Morgan Bukovec, *Finding a Place of My Own*, 2020, Collage, Doug + Laurie Kanyer Art Collection

John Gall, *Untitled*, 2017, Collage on Vintage Photograph, Doug + Laurie Kanyer Art Collection

BASIC DEFINITIONS

GEM

A Gem—for this book—is one of the 125 ways collage transforms emotions and life experiences.

POTENT (EMOTIONAL) EVENT

A potent (emotional) event is an experience that is weighty, or heavy enough, that it elicits a reaction by the systems of the brain causing a behavioral and emotional response. Many events in a person's life register little, if any, behavioral or emotional reaction. A potent event is noticed by the brain systems, causing a reaction based on the importance each person individually places on the experience. Potent emotional events can bring forth a positive or negative reaction. The potent event reactions displayed are the primary emotions consisting of happy, sad, mad, scared, or love. Collage can help to transform these experiences and support the expression of emotions attached to a potent event.

EMOTIONS

Many people use the terms emotions and feelings synonymously. Although you can experience them at the same time, they are not interchangeable. Emotions are physical reactions to an event. They are connected to the release of chemicals called neurotransmitters (oxytocin, epinephrine/adrenaline, cortisol, dopamine, norepinephrine, serotonin, GABA). Neurotransmitters are released into the body, alerting you to pay attention to something. Emotions are physical, bodily responses that come before feelings. Emotions are then expressed through feelings. You will be able to document your emotions and consider them as you make collage.

FEELINGS

Different than emotions, feelings are the responses generated in connection to an emotional event. Feelings are a cognitive thought process in relation to an event ignited by an emotion. A feeling is associated with a series of things such as memories, past experiences, and what is taking place in the present. A feeling begins the process of thinking and decision making related to the event that triggered the emotions. Making collages can help you to explore your feelings and use them as transformational tools toward decision-making and problem-solving.

Note: You can experience more than one emotion and feeling at the same time.

PRIMARY EMOTIONS

There are two types of emotions—primary and secondary. Primary emotions are the first response or reaction to something. The five primary emotions are happy, sad, mad, scared, or love.

SECONDARY EMOTIONS

Secondary emotions are the responses to the primary emotions. Secondary emotions are often complex. For example, you may feel mad (primary) about something and mortified (secondary) about the situation. Secondary emotions tend to linger and become more intense over time.

Collage will help you to learn the difference between primary and secondary emotions. You will gain perspective as you make your collage, allowing you to explore and unearth the secondary emotions and discover what you are really feeling.

Sarah Jarrett, *Inner Gardens*, 2020, Digital Collage, Doug + Laurie Kanyer Art Collection

FEELING RULES

Cultural, family, and social conditioning establish the rules that influence how people in the group express feelings. Often the rules are unspoken as they are modeled in behavior. These rules can lead you to use one feeling when you really mean another, keeping you from saying how you feel. Utilizing collage you can decide and revise the feeling rules that work for you.

FEELING TONES

Tone in art refers to lightness or darkness in a picture. The amount of lightness or darkness in a picture sets an expressive feeling tone and contributes to the mood of the image. It is in many ways the same for feelings. Feeling tone is connected to an affect—the wide range of ways people express feelings in reaction to an experience. A feeling tone is the shade of a feeling being exhibited by the person's affect. It can be light or dark, emotive or restricted. For the purpose of this book, making a collage will help to deepen your awareness of your feeling tone. In using collage you will be able to consider your patterns of feeling tones and explore alternatives.

MOODS

Moods are long lasting feeling tone episodes that can take place over many days. They are often not clearly associated with a specific event and not easily linked to a particular situation. You can explore and gain insight into your moods with collage.

TRUE SELF

Your True Self is the original you at your birth. Using collage will help reacquaint you with your True Self. Collage will allow you to transform your life experiences to discover more about the real, true you.

STERBs

STERBs are short-term, energy-relieving behaviors that people use to defer the potency of pain or discomfort associated with an emotion caused by a potent event. STERBs can be anything one chooses to focus on or use to distract oneself from strong feelings. It is vital to know they will deflect the pain or discomfort, but only for a SHORT period of time. Russell Friedman, who coined the term, also documented that STERBs often become compulsive and addictive. STERBs can add more hardship to the original pain. An example is an illness brought on by smoking. Behaviors like overeating, smoking, alcohol/drug abuse, excessive excerise, excessive shopping, workaholism, cutting one self, overspending, or gambling can have harmful outcomes overtime. STERBs are a form of self medicating to cope with emotional hardships (Friedman, 2009). Collage can be a positive and powerfully productive alternative to using STERBs to manage one's emotional strain

COLLAGE

The original definition of collage comes from the Greek word *kolla* (to glue). This evolved into the French word *collage*. Thus, the act of making art by gluing elements to something is to collage—much like using paint on a canvas is painting. For the purpose of this book, collage is defined not only as an art medium, but as a tool used to transform emotional well-being and enhance self-awareness.

COLLAGIST

Collagist is the term to describe people who are deeply involved in the making of collage. Some might say, collage artist, but I prefer the word collagists as I feel it is a more respectful term. This defines both the professional and hobbyist. Those who paint are not called paint artists; they are called painters.

SUBSTRATE

A substrate is the foundation on which the collage is built. This is often a heavy-weight, acid-free material. It is a good idea to use acid-free paper as a substrate, as it will be stable and last for many years to come. A substrate can be anything you choose, large or small, three-dimensional, or flat. All the elements for the collage are glued onto the substrate.

Axelle Kieffer, *Confinement Fever*, 2020, Collage, Doug + Laurie Kanyer Art Collection

SOURCE MATERIALS

Source material is simply the array of books, magazines, letters, postcards, and/or photographs from which elements are cut or torn, to make a collage.

ELEMENTS

An element is a single-paper item or image found in a book or magazine (source material) that is cut out and then glued to the substrate. It could be a picture of a dog, a house, or a baby—each is considered a single element. It could also be any object you choose to use like a shell, a pebble, a lock of hair. Usually, there are many elements in each collage.

MIXED MEDIA

Mixed media refers to a collage created using other types of art materials in addition to the paper elements. Materials like pencils, crayons, markers, and/or paint, result in a mixed-media collage.

DECOLLAGE

Decollage is the process of tearing away or partially removing elements previously glued to the substrate to reveal the layer (or layers) below. People use their fingers, or tweezers, or a dull dinner knife to dig into the layers of the collage. This is a wonderful metaphor of exploring memories.

Margarita Vera, *Desde mi balcón*, 2020, Digital Collage, Doug + Laurie Kanyer Art Collection

Nina Fraser, *Cut*, 2016, Collage, Doug + Laurie Kanyer Art Collection

Anne Misfeldt, *HEROES*, 2020, Collage, Doug + Laurie Kanyer Art Collection

Let's Begin to Collage

"We collage ourselves into being, finding the pieces of a worldview
and people to love and reasons to live and then integrate
them into a whole, a life consistent with
its beliefs and desires, at least
if we're lucky."

—Rebecca Solnit

SETTING UP TO MAKE COLLAGE & SUGGESTED MATERIALS

YOUR WORKSPACE

You will need to decide on where to set up your collage workspace. There's no need to be elaborate. It just needs to be a comfortable spot to sit and make your collages; a table and a chair. If you like to move around to a variety of places to collage, simply find a box large enough to hold a stack of magazines, scissors, glue, and some substrates. I use my dining room table from time to time. You can find underneath the tablecloth, hidden from view, numerous collages in process.

METHODS AND TECHNIQUES

You might feel you need a bit of technical instruction. I recommend that you refer to the Resource list at the back of the book. These are my suggestions of publications you can borrow or purchase showing you some techniques. You can also find ideas by doing a bit of research on the internet. There are many straight forward, yet imaginative ways to make collage. Learning some steps will help you to proceed with confidence, increasing your enjoyment. You do not need to have special artistic skills to make collages.

MATERIALS

Gather your materials! You will need a pair of scissors, glue, scotch tape, and some old magazines or books. You can use paint, pens, magic markers, a tiny nub of a pencil from under the couch, or your kid's broken crayons. You can genuinely use whatever you come up with in your collages. Feel free to make homemade glue from flour and water, if you want.

USE A SUBSTRATE OF ANY SIZE OR SHAPE

Your collages can be large, super tiny, or somewhere in between. The scale you choose is entirely up to you. Any size substrate you decide to use to address emotions and life events will fit. It is important to know you can use more than just flat-surfaced paper elements to make your collages. You can make them three-dimensional. For example: use a cereal box or a paper cup as a substrate. I have used match boxes, lids from disposable coffee cups—even a small stool.

USE WHATEVER ELEMENTS YOU DESIRE

Keep in mind that the elements—those things you cut out and use in your collage—do not have to be exact representations of the subject matter you are addressing. They can also be symbolic and can be understood and defined by you alone.

The workspace of collagist Monique Vettraino

Sabine Remy, *Einzel-Ausgabe / Single Edition*, 2020, Collage, Doug + Laurie Kanyer Art Collection

USING THE TRIANGLE

TRY STARTING AND ENDING WITH A TRIANGLE

Each time you sit down to make a collage, I suggest you consider placing a triangle shape as the first element you glue down on the substrate. When you come to an ending spot in the collage, consider finishing it by adding another triangle shape. This predictable ritual will help to set a unifying pattern on all the collages you make. It will be a signal that you are engaging in a special time of meditation and transformational collage-making.

Using the triangle at the beginning and the ending of your collage will offer you a familiar and comforting rhythm. Similar to the sun, the moon, and the stars; the triangle will be your grounding symbol. See the list on page 25 that shows all the historical meanings of the triangle; choose one, or more, that symbolizes your journey to help center your creative energy and give you power to navigate your life.

Placing a triangle on your substrate as you begin to make a collage will signal to you that you are doing important work—making it with consideration, reverence, honor, and deep respect. As you cut out a triangle using the paper in the source material you will also bring forth the power, meaning, and strength historically associated with the triangle. You do not have to find an actual triangle element, simply find a section in your source material with a pattern you like and cut a triangle shape.

ABOUT THE POWERFUL TRIANGLE

For centuries humans have used symbols to ignite and inspire higher truths and values. These symbols are like personal shields, touchstones of strength, and inspiration. Symbols have also been used for centuries to represent people in groups with similar values as a unifying emblem. Every important human effort or endeavor seems to have a symbol to represent it; such as Scottish clan tartans, family crests, flags of the nations, and sports team logos. These are icons that inspire and remind people of higher principles in life. They are usually simple in presentation and easy to discern, recall, and remember.

The triangle is one such symbol that has deep historical significance in many cultures and is universally seen as representing the intersection and connection of the meaning of threes. Each side of the triangle represents one of three connected and interdependent tenets. The triangle is also the strongest of shapes—withstanding almost any pressure, nearly impossible to break. It is much like what I refer to as your True Self, the original you at your very birth. Well-known architect R. Buckminster Fuller proved the triangle would withstand twice as much pressure as the rectangle. He based his geodesic shelters on triangles, giving the structures unprecedented strength.

USING THE TRIANGLE COMBATS DRAMA

Dr. Steven Karpman designed a social behavior model called the Drama Triangle.The Drama Triangle was designed to illustrate how human communication patterns can be destructive, causing pain and suffering. It uses the three points of the triangle to demonstrate unhelpful patterns of communication. Karpman chose the term drama as a metaphor to show the roles people use, like actors in play, causing pain and hardship for one another. The three roles are Victim (poor me), Rescuer (let me help you), and Persecutor (it's your fault) (Graham, L. n.d.)

Kellette Elliott, *Triangle*, 2021, Collage, Doug + Laurie Kanyer Art Collection

Karpman's thesis noted that, in order to survive and thrive, people need recognition from others. To receive strokes (units of recognition), to feel alive and of value, people will step into the drama triangle to get their needs for belonging and attention met. If people do not get healthy recognition (positive strokes) from others, they will choose alternative recognition (negative strokes). No one wants to be a zero, to not matter, to be nothing to others.

Karpman's Drama Triangle starts as someone plays the role of victim or persecutor. Eventually another person is invited to join in the conflict and drama. What is remarkable is the actors in the Drama Triangle move and change positions. They begin to take on the others' roles as the drama unfolds. It is as if they are playing a dangerous interpersonal game to gain recognition, power, and control. The result is pain, and the pattern of interpersonal interaction results in suffering.

Another behavioral theory using the triangle as an illustration to explain the actions of people was created by Murray Bowen. Bowen invented the theory of Triangulation in 1966. This concept is related to the notion that when two people are experiencing some upset or strain between them, in order to manage and in an attempt to decrease the intensity, they will invite another person to get involved (Jones, 2020). The process of getting people to come into the triangle is called Triangulation, and it is a form of manipulation (Jones, 2020).

What Triangulation does is move the focus away from the two original people who had the problem. Triangulation spreads out the depth and weight of stress between the original two and attempts to involve another. While the third person had no role initially, they are invited into the strain so that the stress can be deferred onto them. Sadly, when this happens, the one invited into the conflict can become entangled and drama can increase for all. The original problem between the two does not get amended when Triangulation is used. It is a no-win situation resulting in confusion and chaos.

THERE IS GOOD NEWS—AN ALTERNATIVE

By adopting one or more honorable historical meanings of the Triangle one can avoid, rather than enter into the drama. When facing an invitation to enter into drama, you will have the power to choose to rise above and invest in a higher level of function by making a collage about it. As you read this book you will be confronted, in many of the Gems, to consider the drama and hardships in your past. You will begin and end with a triangle representing one or more of its positive historical meanings when you make collages on the topics of the Gems. In doing so you will impose upon yourself an alternative to drama and you will be able to adopt and operate with higher character traits. In doing so you will have the power and strength to recognize and oppose any invitation to jump onto the Drama Triangle others may invite you to join.

In making collage, using a new definition of the triangle, you will be able to see with greater acuity the games people play and how drama unfolds. You can then choose to send out transformational energy of love, respect and honor toward them, rather than enter into Triangulation or to jump onto the Drama Triangle. You can gain and have possession of deeper wisdom, to avoid conflict in the present day and transform your emotions and life experiences from the past.

TRIANGLE—A GROUNDING BEACON

The triangle is an excellent shape for you to consider using as you begin to explore the Gems and make your collages. Think of it as a grounding beacon toward deeper self-awareness. As you use the Gems in the book the triangle will be the unifying symbol in all the collages you make. Using a triangle can be your personal symbol, an emblem of strength, and mark of perseverance for this journey. In some ways, this triangle can be like a lighthouse showing you the way.

HISTORICAL MEANINGS OF THE TRIANGLE

Beginning, Middle, Ending
Past, Present, Future
Waxing, Waning, Full Moon
Body, Mind, Spirit
Acceptance, Understanding, Appreciation
Mother, Maiden, Crone
Thoughts, Feelings, Emotions
Love, Truth, Wisdom
Woman, Man, Child
Strength, Care, Courage
Sun, Moon, Stars
Left, Right, Center
Life, Death, Rebirth

Stream, River, Ocean
Create, Revise, Sustain
Earth, Air, Sky
Serenity, Courage, Wisdom
Head, Heart, Intuition
Earth, Wind, Fire
Father, Son, Holy Ghost
Manifestation, Enlightenment, Revelation
Physical, Mental, Spiritual
Unity, Service, Recovery
Three choices / wishes in traditional fairy tales
Strength of the three-strand braid
Strength of the three-strand cord

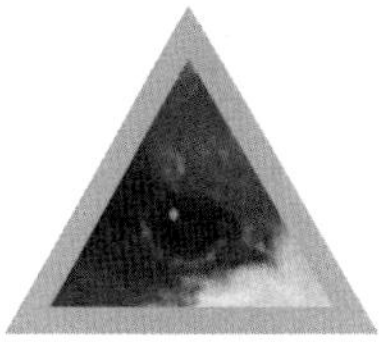

START WHEN YOU ARE READY

YOU ARE IN CHARGE

The process of considering your feelings, life experiences, and relationships is a relatively potent and tender thing to do—take your time. Let the ideas in this book marinate. Sit with them a bit, offering yourself time to ponder and consider. Avoid pressure and perfection. You have time—there is no rush.

YOU HAVE DONE BRAVE THINGS BEFORE

Begin to cut and paste when you are ready. Remember you have done new, brave things in your life. As you begin to explore collage, bring forth the courage it took to enter a new classroom each year as a child, or to show up for the first day of a new job as an adult. You have within you the power to explore your emotions and life experiences with collage.

BE GENTLE—PACE YOURSELF—JUST CUT AND PASTE TO BEGIN YOUR TRANSFORMATION

Remember, you are not trying to make a masterpiece, so the pressure is off! You do not have to show your collage to anyone. Just make collage as an act of self-love and respect. Like brushing your teeth, creating a collage will help you feel better and potentially head off future problems, such as a toothache. The act alone of cutting and pasting is relaxing and reduces stress, too.

Think of making a collage for the first time as if you are going to a new exercise class or attending a workshop on a topic of interest to you. You begin slowly, right? You show up (have this book in your hands), observe others (see the collages featured in the book), listen to the cues from the instructor (read the information in the book) and give it a try (make a collage). Continue to make more collages to build deeper emotional awareness, strength, and insight as you consider your life experience.

SUGGESTED BEGINNING STEPS

- **Step One:** Turn to the CONTENTS page of the book, and locate Part 3: 125 Gems of Truth - Evidence of How Collage Transforms. Then, scan and read all the Gem topic categories.
- **Step Two:** Locate a Gem topic that resonates with you right now—one you can apply to your life. Turn to the page of the Gem topic that appeals to you. Example; Gems Reducing Stress, page 77.
- **Step Three:** Once you are on the page of the Gem topic you want to explore, read the titles of all the Gems to find exactly the Gem you really connect with today. Let's say; Gem 33 Collage Offers a Needed Escape on page 78.
- **Step Four:** Read the Gem. When you are ready use the material in the Gem as a prompt to make a collage. This will begin your journey toward transforming how this topic affects your life.
- **Step Five:** Start and end your collage with a triangle shape representing one or more of the historical meaning on page 25. Also, consider adding a deliberate error as discussed on page 28.
- **Step Six:** End the entire transformational experience by using the Final Action Steps on page 30.
- **Step Seven:** In the future, use the Gems as a meditative or collage process or to gather information to support your transformational journey. Use the *Collage Care* Gems topics and materials to transform your thinking, feelings, and happenings in life.

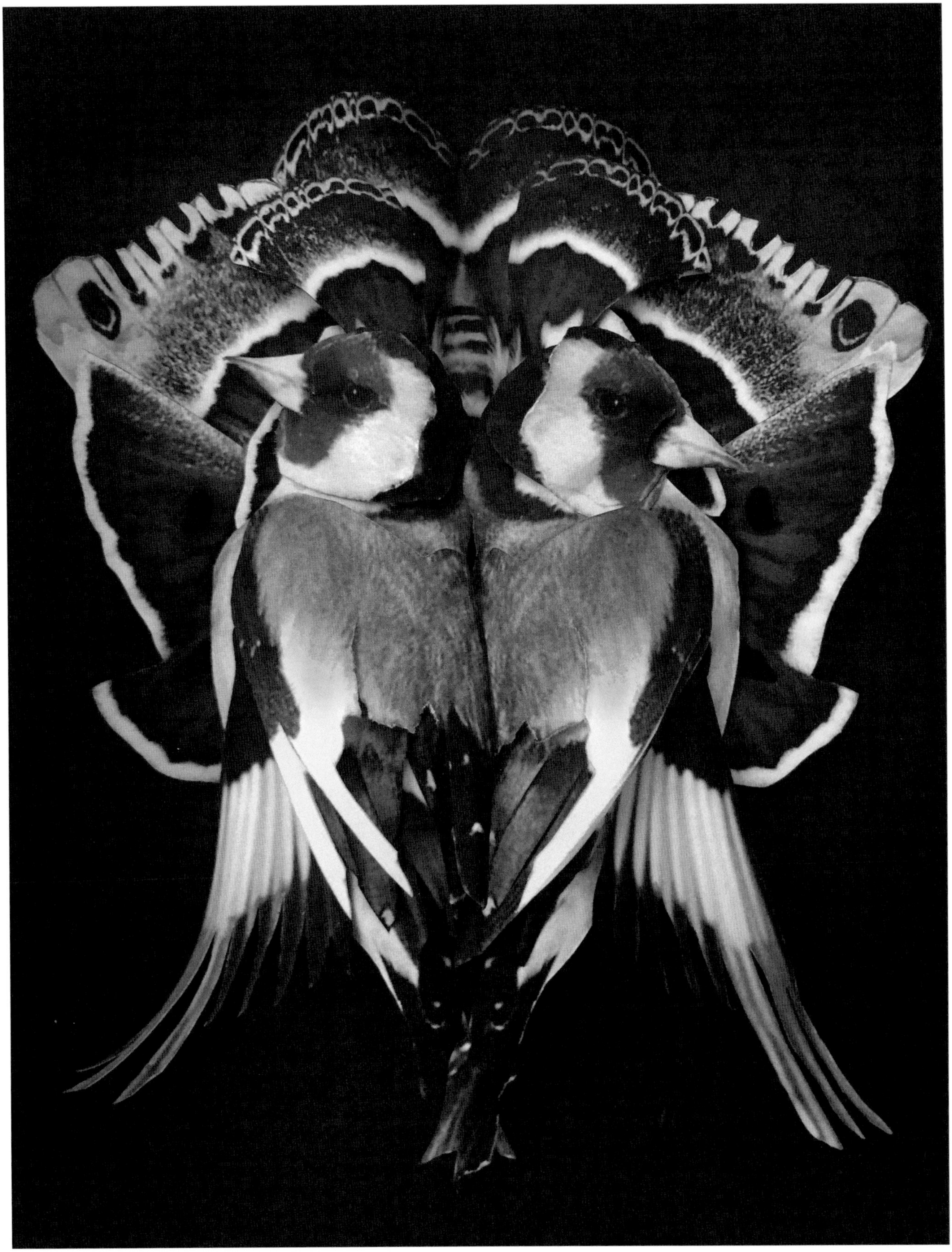

Sarah Best, *Anima Falcondidae*, 2020, Mixed Media Collage with Sculpted Paper, Doug + Laurie Kanyer Art Collection

DELIBERATE ERRORS & EXTENDING GRACE

As you begin to make collages you may be confronted with an invitation towards perfectionism. While it is honorable to do an excellent job, perfectionism can become toxic and disabling. It often creeps into anxiety, obsessive compulsions, and then into procrastination. For many, the possibility of shame being projected upon them for not being perfect is too big of a risk to take. They subsequently find themselves cemented in prolonged episodes of procrastination. They discover themselves nervous and hesitant to complete a project, prolonging and avoiding the judgment of others. Judgment carries with it punishment. The punishment is often shame. Their dreams—held captive in the prison of perfectionism. Most all of this is done outside one's awareness.

There is a myth connected to a number of cultures of a tradition where creative souls make a deliberate error in their rugs or quilts, so as to not offend God. I would add, to not offend others, too. Why make a deliberate error? So as to not claim to be perfect, to be better than others, or to bring on potential criticism, embarrassment or shame when a error is discovered.

I suggest, in making your collage that you add a deliberate error. Once you have placed your beginning triangle element on your collage, your next step could be to make an intentional error. Let's agree for you to accept the work here of making collage to transform, is not about making a perfect masterpiece collage. Consider, is the expression of emotions perfect? This work is for you, in all your humanness to use the tool of collage to transform your emotions and life experiences. *Collage is a process here, not a product.*

To get the temptation to be perfect out of the way, make a deliberate error. Find and discover some off, random, deliberate, something of an element, that has no connection or relationship to the topic you aim to explore. Cut or tear it out of your source material and place it on your collage. Make an initial random error and get the mistake over with. Put it there in your collage to embrace your utter and most wonderful imperfection. Do so to walk on a path of extending grace to yourself—to embrace your humanness.

In this same spirit and tradition myself and the senior book designer have left an intentional error—while we likely have left many. We left one we know of, that mingles with all the errors we made that we don't know of—the ones you will find as you read. In doing so we readily admit, embrace, and recognize this book is not perfect. When you find an error in this book, (note the intentional error is embedded in one of the Gem titles), pause to radiate your most precious, deep grace and forgiveness towards us and then radiate it to yourself. Reflect on the notion that rather than not closing the circle—avoiding the launch of this book, for fear of it not being perfect—we slayed that dragon of perfection and all its associated potential shame by acknowledging and embracing our errors.

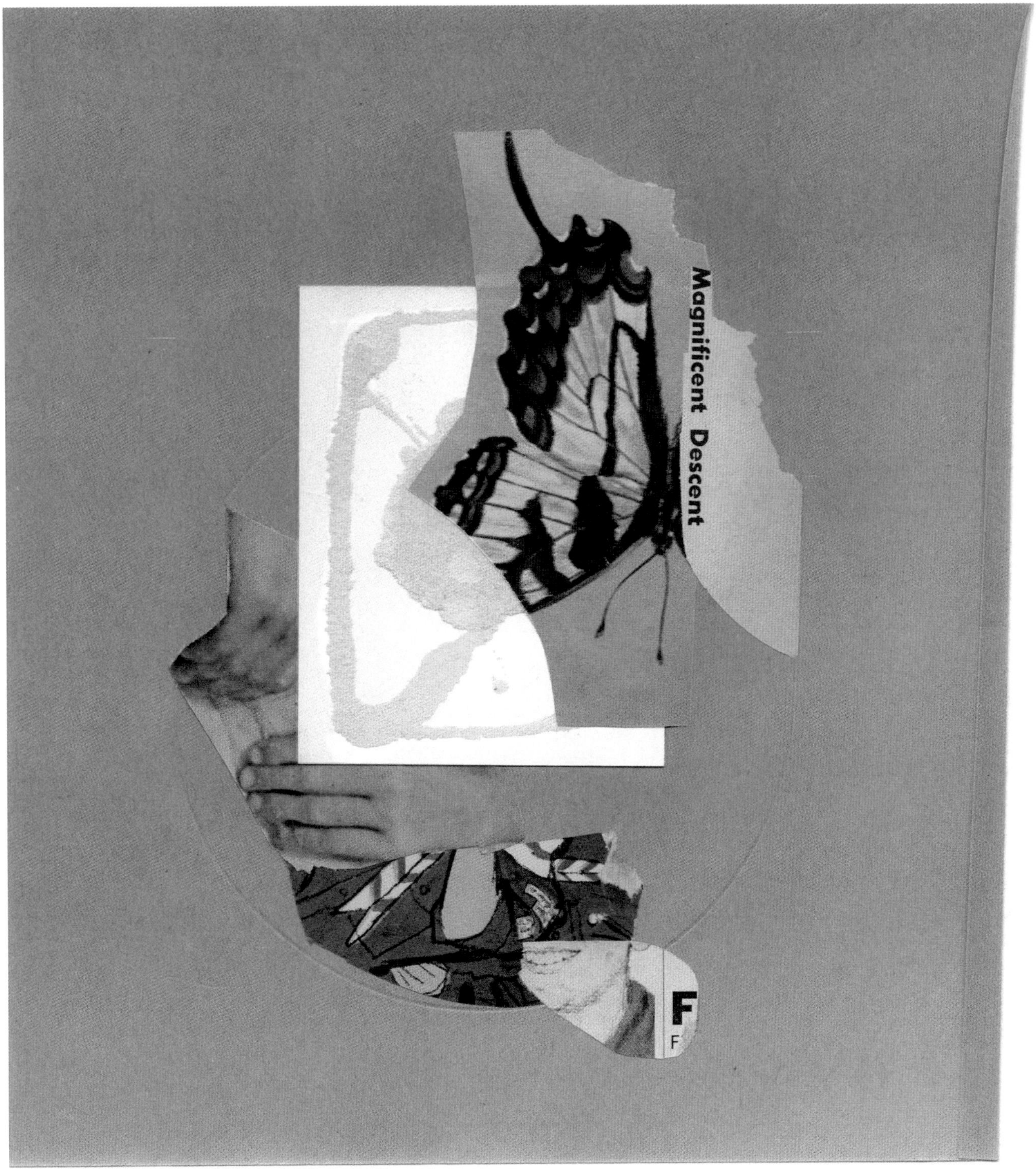

Fred Free, *often a surprise*, 2019, Collage, Doug + Laurie Kanyer Art Collection

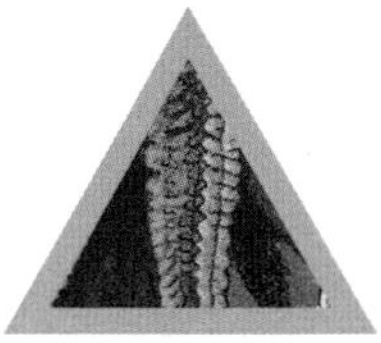

ACTION STEPS FOR FINAL TRANSFORMATION

To extend your collage transformation take some time to deepen the experience with these action steps.

Write on the back of your collage or make additional collages to answer the questions below.

QUESTIONS TO PONDER AND ASK YOURSELF

What do I feel now having completed my collage?

How have my feelings changed from before I made my collage?

What did I notice?

What did I learn?

What have I decided?

How have I changed my mind or revised a life decision?

What behavioral patterns do I notice that need to be changed in my life?

What other information do I need?

What do I need to do now?

Who might I need to talk to about this?

What will I remember for the future?

Is there a date I need to establish to take any next steps?

Who can I connect with for more information, assistance, help, or encouragement?

WRITE OR COLLAGE A SUPPORTIVE THOUGHT

On the back of your collage write or glue some symbolic elements to create a supportive thought fortifying your new learning and awareness.

You might write your supportive thought and then make a collage that responds to it.

You can also choose to cut out word elements to create your supportive thought.

Examples:

"I can explore my feelings and use them to help me solve problems."

"I can decide for myself what works best for me."

"My loving memories can be cherished and offer me strength."

"I can think for myself."

"I can think and feel at the same time."

"My life challenges are opportunities to solve problems, gather information, and make new decisions."

"I can change my mind and revise my earlier conclusions."

"I can use my feelings as cues to get my needs met and solve problems."

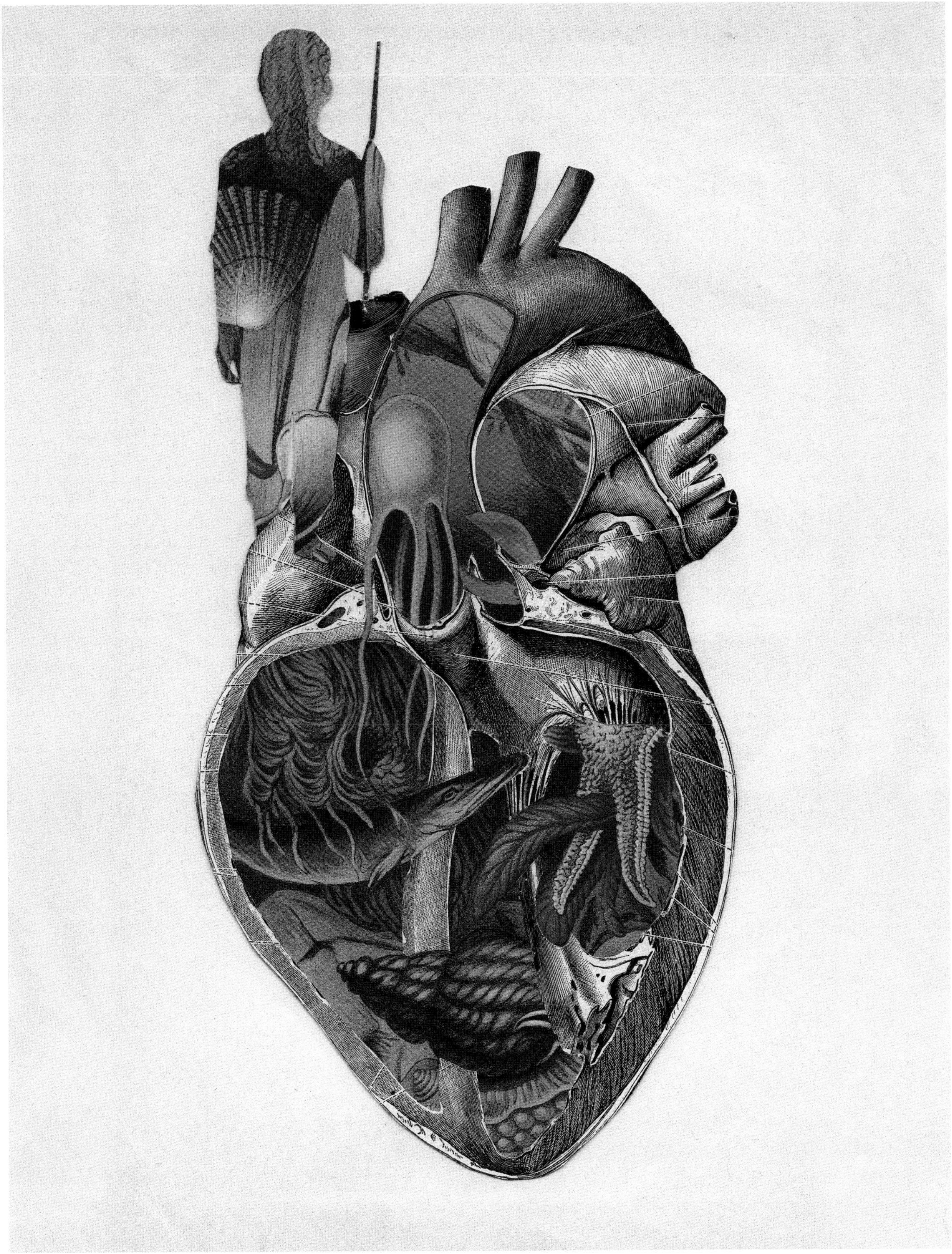

Kevin Geronimo Brandtner, *Heart Tank*, 2019, Collage, Doug + Laurie Kanyer Art Collection

AUTHOR'S NOTE

YOU ARE WHOLE

The field of psychology is relatively new. The first psychology laboratory was opened by Wilhelm Wundt 1879 and the legendary Austrian neurologist, Sigmund Freud, only began his formal practice specializing in brain disorders in 1886. Although scientists are working hard to deepen our understanding of the brain, we still have a long way to go to overcome bias and ignorance related to brain health. In the meantime, people who struggle with their emotions or relationships are often called broken and dysfunctional. Consider—you would never label a person with high blood pressure as broken or dysfunctional!

The brain, the heart, the lungs, and the kidneys are all just organs. People who are navigating anxiety, depression, post-traumatic stress disorder, prolonged grief, and family or love/relationship concerns are not broken. They are struggling with hardships related to functions of the brain, to thinking, feeling and decision-making. No wonder people have a hard time recovering when others see them in such poor light.

I believe all people, regardless of their level of current functioning, have strengths and they are whole. While undoubtedly the brain or relationship under strain can cause challenges that might require time to ferret out and resolve, people experiencing emotional unrest are no more broken than people with cancer. Yes, you may have an illness related to the brain organ, but you are not broken! You are a whole person facing difficulties. Most symptoms and manifestations of emotions and relationships that cause behavioral unrest can improve. This is also true for those whose concerns may be connected to a genetically-seeded, emotional trauma.

Although we have a way to go in the field of psychology and communication, those working on the study of the brain are making advances and we have evidence-based modalities of treatment that help facilitate recovery. I am here to challenge the labels and discriminatory language people use to describe others with emotional hardships and interpersonal struggles. It has been my experience that collage is a powerful tool that can be part of the solution.

In the care of all bodily organs, the brain included, there are things to do to improve their function—to address the concerns. This book offers insight on how collage is one way to address the transformation of your emotions, thoughts, and relationships. Within these pages, you will discover you are strong and capable even while experiencing a hiccup emotionally or relationally. You will be able to see the truth that you are whole.

Please know that you are not, nor have ever been, broken and dysfunctional. You are whole, capable and profoundly created to find peace and connection in your life.

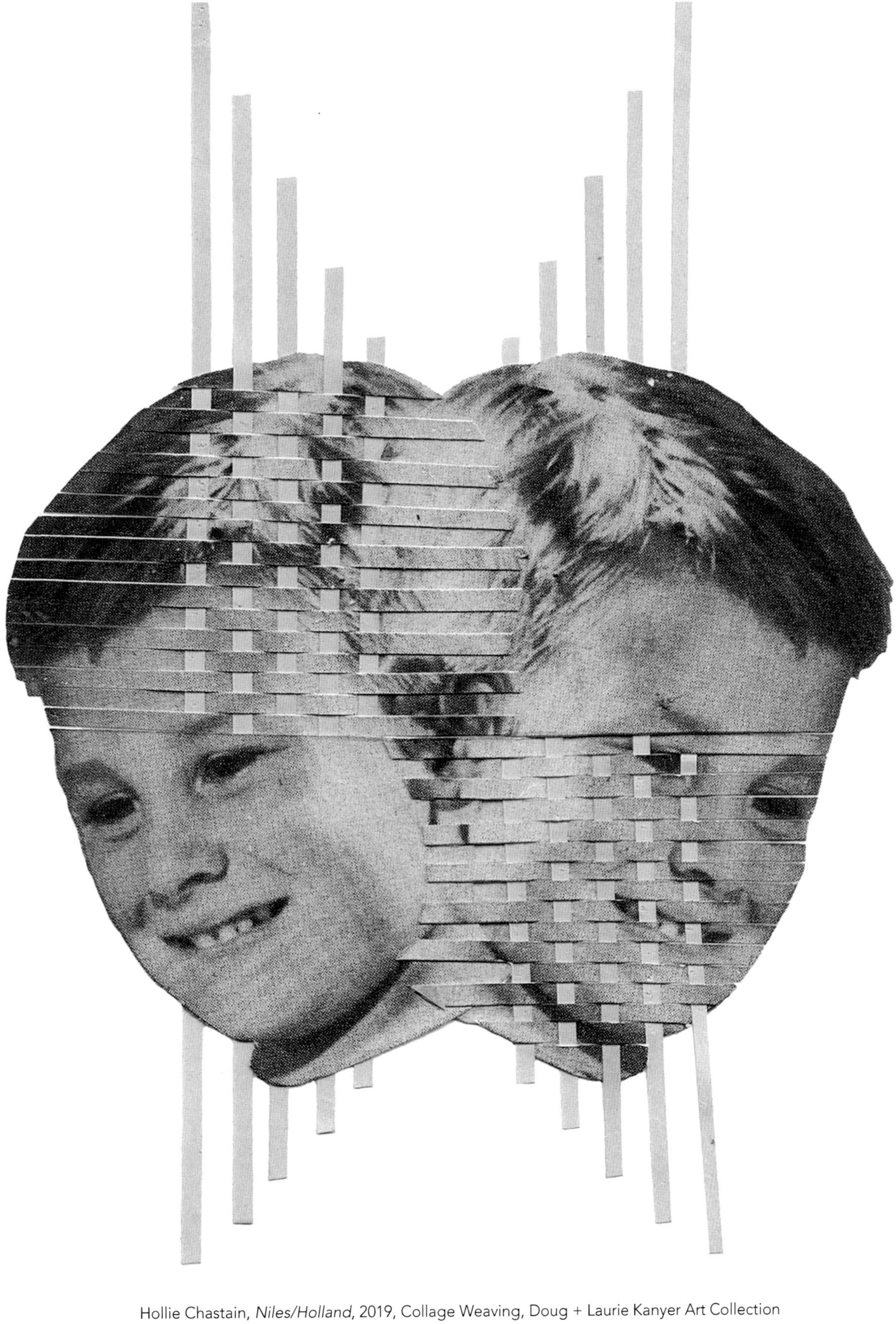

Hollie Chastain, *Niles/Holland*, 2019, Collage Weaving, Doug + Laurie Kanyer Art Collection

SELF-LOVE

The notion of self-awareness, self-care, and self-love is not a concept promoting the elevation of self over others. Rather, it is to intentionally care for yourself to be able to experience a full, satisfying life, and to be able to actively participate in community and the care of other people. When you are living a life where you are addressing and transforming stressful emotions and experiences, rather than stuffing them or indulging in hurtful distractions (STERBs), you will be able to flourish and contribute to other's welfare, too. Self-love ensures you will be able to live a full and productive life—to be healthy, capable of tending to yourself and then be able to serve others.

You need tools to help reduce any sticky, heavy, stressful, or straining emotional event. The uncomfortable residue from a potent emotional or stressful experience can cause you to be less fruitful and can affect your perception of the world. Collage can help you help yourself! In this way making a collage is an act of self-care, leading to self-awareness, and demonstrates self-love that leads to the ability to love and care for others.

One way to look at it is to imagine yourself on an airplane. Suddenly, there is enough turbulence that the emergency air bags are released. It is vital for you to first tend to your own oxygen needs (self-care) and then to assist others. If you are breathing and functioning (tending to you self-care) you will live, and therefore be able to help others survive.

When you make collages to address potent emotions and weighty life experiences, it is as if you are on the plane with sudden, unexpected disturbances. As you make the collage, it is as if you are taking in clean-flowing-air during an inflight incident. By making a collage to address stressors you will then be well enough—having the strength to move forward—to be able to help others who need assistance. The alternative could be devastating!

Collage is a useful tool to consider your emotions and life events so you can understand them, minimize the effect of negative circumstances on your system, and then move on, avoiding the taxing effects of hardships. This is far from being selfish and self absorbed. It is practical and wise to invest in self-care, self-awareness, and self-love. Making a collage has the healing capacity to bring forth protection, strength, insight, and health for you that naturally pours over to others.

Janice McDonald, *Beat*, 2016, Collage, Doug + Laurie Kanyer Art Collection

Irie Wata, *Sanctuary*, 2021, Digital Collage, Doug + Laurie Kanyer Art Collection

Julie Liger-Belair, *Precarious Balance*, 2020, Collage, Doug + Laurie Kanyer Art Collection

125 Gems of Truth: Evidence of How Collage Transforms

"Collage is a super sensitive and scrupulously accurate
instrument, similar to a seismograph, which is
able to record the exact amount
of the possibility of human
happiness at any
period."

—Max Ernst

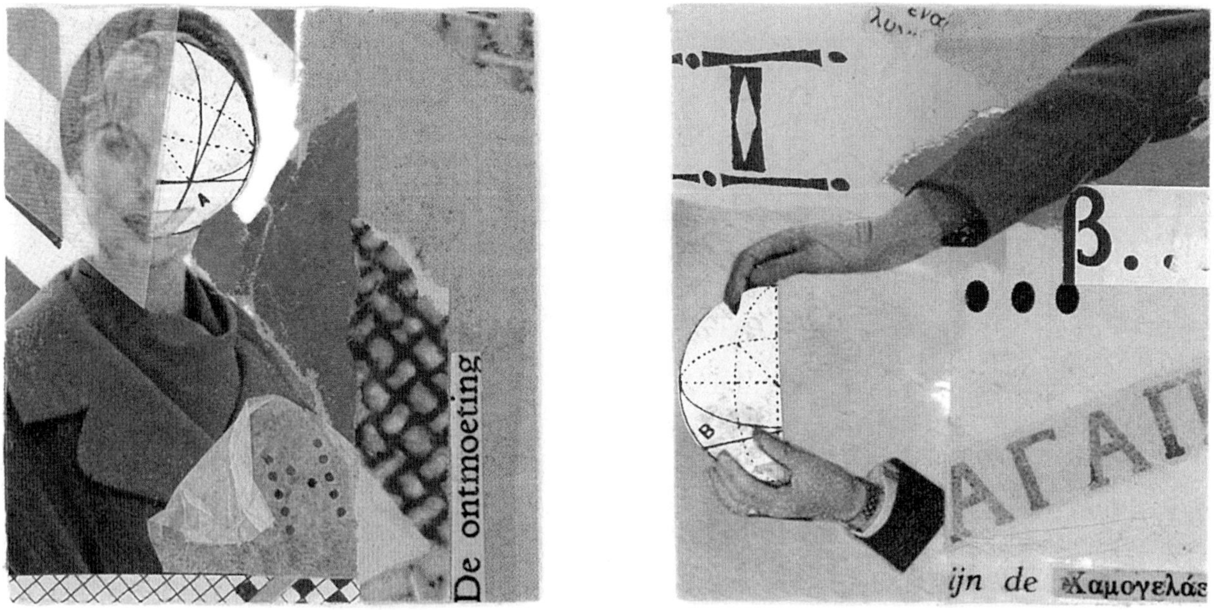

Dorothée Mesander, *From a........to* ***β***, 2020, Mini Collage, Doug + Laurie Kanyer Art Collection

Dorothée Mesander, *I'll Wait for You at the Docks*, 2020, Mini Collage, Doug + Laurie Kanyer Art Collection

What are the Gems?

"Collage is more than just an art style. Collage is all about bringing different elements together. Once you form a sensibility about connection, how different elements relate to each other, you deepen your understanding of yourself and others."

—Bryan Collier

About the Gems

These Gems of truth offer an abundance of ideas on how collage transforms emotions and life experiences. Rather than lengthy chapters, this material is offered in a nugget-like, meditative format.

Each Gem is packed with complex information presented in a simple manner, offering quick access to valuable ideas. You will be able to read and meditate on each Gem and then consider them as evidence of how collage supports emotional health. The hope is that this material will inspire you to use collage to improve your well-being.

I used a gemstone (Gems) as a metaphor to illustrate the profound transformation one goes through in using collage to tend to emotions and life experiences. Gemstones start as rocks. The starting point of their journey toward becoming valuable, sentimental treasures, takes work and dedication. These rocks are put through a process of cutting, polishing, and are eventually placed into a setting created from precious metals. This is what is required for them to become priceless and cherished. So think of the following Gems as transformational actions—polishing, cutting, and setting in gold—that you can do with collage to transform your emotions and life experiences.

As you read the Gems, think of the metaphor of a collage itself. You can use the Gems as you would select elements to construct a collage. When you make a collage, you scan source materials to find elements that fit best for the ideas you are working to create. You then cut each element out, build a pleasing composition, and apply them to your substrate to finish your collage.

Applying the collage process here with the Gems, find the ones you need for your life. Scan the various categories of the Gems, then pick and choose the ones you would like to read. Use the information in those Gems to inform your collage of life—to support your transformation and emotional wellness.

Next to each Gem is a collage made by fine artists whose art is included in the Doug + Laurie Kanyer Art Collection. The inclusion of the collages serves a number of purposes. The collages offer a focal point to rest your eyes as you consider the Gem you have just read. They are therapeutic, just as gazing on art inspires, challenges, and comforts. In many cases the subject of the collage matches the subject of the Gem—the collage serves to illustrate the topic of the Gem. The inclusion of the collages also aims to show you a variety of ways collage can be made. These collages expose you to the greater world, as they are created by artists from every corner of the earth. Lastly, this is the first time we have shown our collages in print, so you are having a private showing of the Collection.

Choose a Gem that works for you (*think, choose, and use*) and then make a collage. Approach this material with the curiosity you might have when embarking on a new adventure. Make collages and apply the wisdom of the Gems to transform your emotions and life experiences.

Donna Morello, *Poppy Zipper*, 2020, Collage with Zipper, Doug + Laurie Kanyer Art Collection

Mark Watkins, *Making it Better*, 2020, Collage, Doug + Laurie Kanyer Art Collection

Gems Illustrating How Collage is for Everyone & Supports Well-Being

"Every human being is an artist, a freedom being,
called to participate in transforming and
reshaping the conditions, thinking
and structures that shape
and inform our
lives."

—Joseph Beuyers

GEM 1 ▷ **Collage Opens Access to Everyone**

Collage is affordable and accessible to people of all ages, incomes, and skill levels. All that is necessary is a pair of scissors, glue, and a stack of old magazines or books. There is no need for extensive training or costly art supplies because most collage materials are affordable or free! Unlike other art forms, collage is inherently democratic and inclusive. You will not be sidelined by an absence of resources or past experiences of making art.

Simply find a comfortable spot at your dining room table and begin making collage instantly. You can use any paper you have in your space. Magazines are a classic go-to for source material. Loaded with expressive images and bold words, magazines are perfect for exploring feelings and experiences. Ask around, people will gladly share their leftover periodicals with you. To keep expenses down, one convenient and thrifty alternative to purchasing glue is to make wheat paste. Simply mix flour and water to glue the elements of your collage onto your substrate. You can use tape too. Collage is an accessible art form and welcomes you with open arms. Everyone can benefit from making a collage!

GEM 2 ▷ **Collage Eases Expression**

Collage uses ready-made images cut from magazines called elements, offering you a swift way to show feelings. If you have a difficult time with something, you can cut out an element from a magazine to represent the problem. With collage you can show the situation representationally with ease. What you see in this book are fine art collages made by expert artists. To make fine art collages you need refined technical skills, some dedicated practice and study. To use collage to express challenging life events you don't need to have their level of technical skills as you can take an image placing it on collage without considering the artistic aspects a fine artist needs to consider.

With collage, there is no need for hours upon hours of drawing classes or weekends spent in painting workshops. You don't need a fancy studio or a prestigious art degree; you need your hands, your imagination, some affordable materials, and faith in yourself to make that first step. If you know how to use a pair of scissors and a glue stick, you have the skills you need to begin your journey to tell your story! Making collage can be truly that straightforward and immensely rewarding.

GEM 3 ▷ **Collage Confirms We are All Artists**

Each and every one of us is an artist. As poet John O'Donohue said: "We are all involved in the creations of our own world" (Tibbett, n.d.). On a daily basis, we are creating our own life, piecing together the minutes and hours of the day. As you build your life, you surround yourself with objects to uplift, inspire, and define you in your living spaces, at work, and even with what you wear.

You essentially live in a collage of life. You collage with what you do and how you live. Since everything is collage, we are all artists! The items and objects of your life, whether they be something functional or decorative, are expressions of your artistic nuances and references of your living collage. Even the expression of emotions is a creative endeavor!

The object's value is not important, either. It could be a vase you inherited from your grandmother or one you found at a yard sale. What matters is the artistic articulation of your individual creative sensibilities. It does not have to be a leap, really, to embrace and apply writer Chelsea Reed's notions about art. She writes, "Art (objects you live with) not only improves our physical and mental health, it empowers us with a sense of purpose. The creativity that comes with looking at art (or the items you live with

Zoë Charlton, *Hill Country*, 2019, Collage, Doug + Laurie Kanyer Art Collection and love) can change our outlook on life and assure us there are better days ahead. Art provides an escape from the everyday grind" (Reed, 2019). Adopt the thoughts of O'Donohue and Reed. I maintain that all humans are artists and as you collage you will see this to be true. You have remarkable artistic abilities to create on a daily basis, and do so all the time. If you got the impression in your early years that you are not an artist because someone said you could not paint or draw, revise those notions now by making collages. Choose to move beyond your earlier beliefs and adopt collage as a vehicle for your artistic and creative expression.

GEM 4 ▷ Collage Allows You to Be Present for Yourself—Personal Time

You may have been socialized and conditioned to be outwardly focused and look out for others. This collective approach is a wise and necessary social skill in order to have a thriving community. It stems from the belief that if all are strong, then the individual will be strong, too. Maybe though, you have taken that to mean your own needs are not to be considered or that you should sacrifice your own care for others. Maybe you are one who is naturally wired to be the helping type; but, taken too far, you may be neglecting your own well-being.

This neglect stacks up and, before you know it, you find you are far away from yourself, adrift and disconnected from your needs. You may be overlooking the importance of time for yourself, failing to consider the many restorative benefits you gain from personal time. Time to pause, contemplate, and get space from others' demands is vital to emotional health.

You need time to be present with yourself, to let the mind drift and ponder. You might need a pause from focusing on the community. Maybe you need time to show up for yourself and tend to a deeply important relationship with yourself. I knew a therapist who told her clients to become bored in order to find peace.

Making a collage allows you to play a creative Solitaire of sorts—to be with yourself, not by yourself. Know that you are never really alone. In being present for yourself, you demonstrate to yourself you are worthy, wonderful and wanted—yes, wanted by you! This is not selfish. You will be a better helper by being refreshed. You will discover that all of your life you have wanted to know how to spend time with yourself—to be quietly alone with just you.

Time spent making collage is like going on a date with yourself. You will discover more about yourself and come to see yourself as a worthy, remarkable, and a profound being.

GEM 5 ▷ Collage Counsels and Advises

When you are doing well emotionally, you move smoothly through a life event; you regulate your feelings, make sound judgments, consider options, take necessary actions, and then move on. Being in a balanced state, even in the face of a heavy situation, you are able to be your own best counselor. You are able to face the situation by having your own two-way conversation in your head, formulating a response to the event. You are able to successfully modulate your feelings, reactions, and responses; and then move forward.

Even the most proficient in the process of self-counseling will find times when the potency of the event and the related activated feelings cause detours. Times of uncertainty often call for support and help from others. A phone call to a friend helps, a walk in fresh air with a family member can be calming; in some cases, a call to a professional may be indicated.

Margot De Korte, *A Day Full of Color*, 2020, Collage, Doug + Laurie Kanyer Art Collection

Collage can be added to the list of helpers when struggling with hardships. The nature of collage, with its unique formatting mechanisms, may be one of the best problem-solvers—maybe even the best counselor you will ever have. Making a collage offers the opportunity for a new voice to emerge in your internal dialogue.

Note: In addition to using collage, seek quality advisors, friends, and professional counselors alike to help you process emotions, listen to you, reflect back your feelings, as well as assist in labeling and accepting your feelings. They can help to refine your thoughts, consider memories, address behavioral urges, offer feedback, and support a plan to resolve the situation. It is also critical for these helpers to suspend value judgements and provide respect.

GEM 6 ▷ **Collage Explores the Five Finger Rule**

You can make a collage to explore a model I developed to help my clients track their emotional well-being called The Five Finger Rule™. It uses your hand as a model to help you remember the various aspects of caring for your emotional health needs. Each finger on your hand represents one aspect of a good mental health practice and helps you track and remember the things you need to do to feel good emotionally.

Thumb represents physical self-care, such as the right amount of healthy food, exercise, experiencing the outdoors, recreation, relaxation, or drinking water.

Pointer Finger represents social care, such as being around kind people, having a positive work environment, being with a loving family and creating boundaries with social pressure/conditioning.

Middle Finger represents talk therapy, from a trained practitioner utilizing evidence-based modalities to combat destructive patterns and self-talk. In counseling you will learn and practice new skills to address your needs and regulate your emotions.

Ring Finger represents consulting with medical providers to ensure your emotional status is not caused by other physical conditions, such as an autoimmune struggle. In some cases your doctor may prescribe medications to help your emotional status. Many people will need these medications for a temporary time period. Like any medication, report any undue side effects you experience. It is not uncommon to try a few medications to discover the best fit for you. Make sure and consult with a doctor prior to discontinuing any medication.

Pinky Finger represents gathering good, quality, up-to-date information about your condition. Make sure the information is valid by verifying that the sources come from comprehensive research.

Pinky Finger also represents finding support from others who have had similar experiences. Often those who have gone through what you are experiencing will offer encouragement and valuable suggestions.

You can make a collage featuring the various fingers of the Five Finger Rule to track and remind you to give yourself a hand in your own personal well-being.

Jasmine Romero, *Hope*, 2020, Collage, Doug + Laurie Kanyer Art Collection

GEM 7 ▷ **Collage Familiarizes You with Your Internal Dialogue**

Collage offers you the opportunity to explore the internal dialogue occurring in your mind. That little voice in your head consists of the constantly running thoughts that advise, counsel, coach, and help to decipher what is going on around you. This dialogue, known as self-talk, is an internal process. It tells you about both yourself and the world, helping you to navigate while shaping your decisions. It also formulates conclusions about yourself and the situation.

Sometimes the dialogue can be supportive; other times it can confuse your assessment of life experiences and your role within them. Making a collage can help familiarize you with the constant conversation and the conclusions of this little voice in your head. You will be able to consider habitual patterns in your responses to circumstances.

Making a collage about what you say to yourself—about yourself and others—can help you to know more about the accuracy of your internal dialogue. This knowledge may allow you to make the necessary shifts in your thinking or to consider your thoughts more in depth. Collage can reveal your conclusions and help you to see if they are true or need some revision; just like a quality counselor or loyal friend might do.

GEM 8 ▷ **Collage Accesses the Subconscious—Reveals Your Hidden Language**

Your subconscious is the totality of the mental process that operates outside of your awareness. Have you ever sensed trouble brewing or got a hunch in the middle of tackling a dilemma that there was more going on than you realized? It is likely your subconscious trying to clue you in.

Collage enables you to harness this mysterious inside information. It allows your subconscious to rise up and reveal insights into concerns you feel deep within yourself. Over time, you will notice that the collages you make frequently reveal the cause of a problem you are experiencing. Additionally, the collage may expose more about your thoughts and feelings on the matter.

The subconscious is a wise and supportive part of who you are, and it hides deep within. Collages provide a visual vocabulary to communicate the source of your subconscious concerns. As collagist Frances Ryan said, "I make the collage, and then later I can see the story." Hearing this might cause you to pause, maybe feel a bit agitated or uncomfortable, and question what might be exposed. It is natural to feel this way when faced with the unknown. Still, those I know who explored collage as a transformative tool discovered critical insights needed to further progress in problem-solving.

Collage will help you understand what occurred by bringing the problem to light. Like a beacon blazing through the shadows of the subconscious mind, collage will spotlight the problem and illuminate the way to possible solutions. The pathway from subconscious to collage is quite profound.

GEM 9 ▷ **Collage Removes Interpretation**

Suspending judgment and interpretation was a foundational belief in the collage work I did with clients in the past. Collage creates a personal reaction, both within the creator and the viewer. The collage's contents might evoke a viewer's reaction, but that reaction is theirs. What they believe they see has nothing to do with what the collage actually means to you.

I encourage you—as you make collages—to protect yourself from those who aim to project meaning onto your collage. You are invited to make your collage as a way to become curious and learn more about yourself. One way to do this is to make a collage then return later—possibly days later—to see what there is for you to consider.

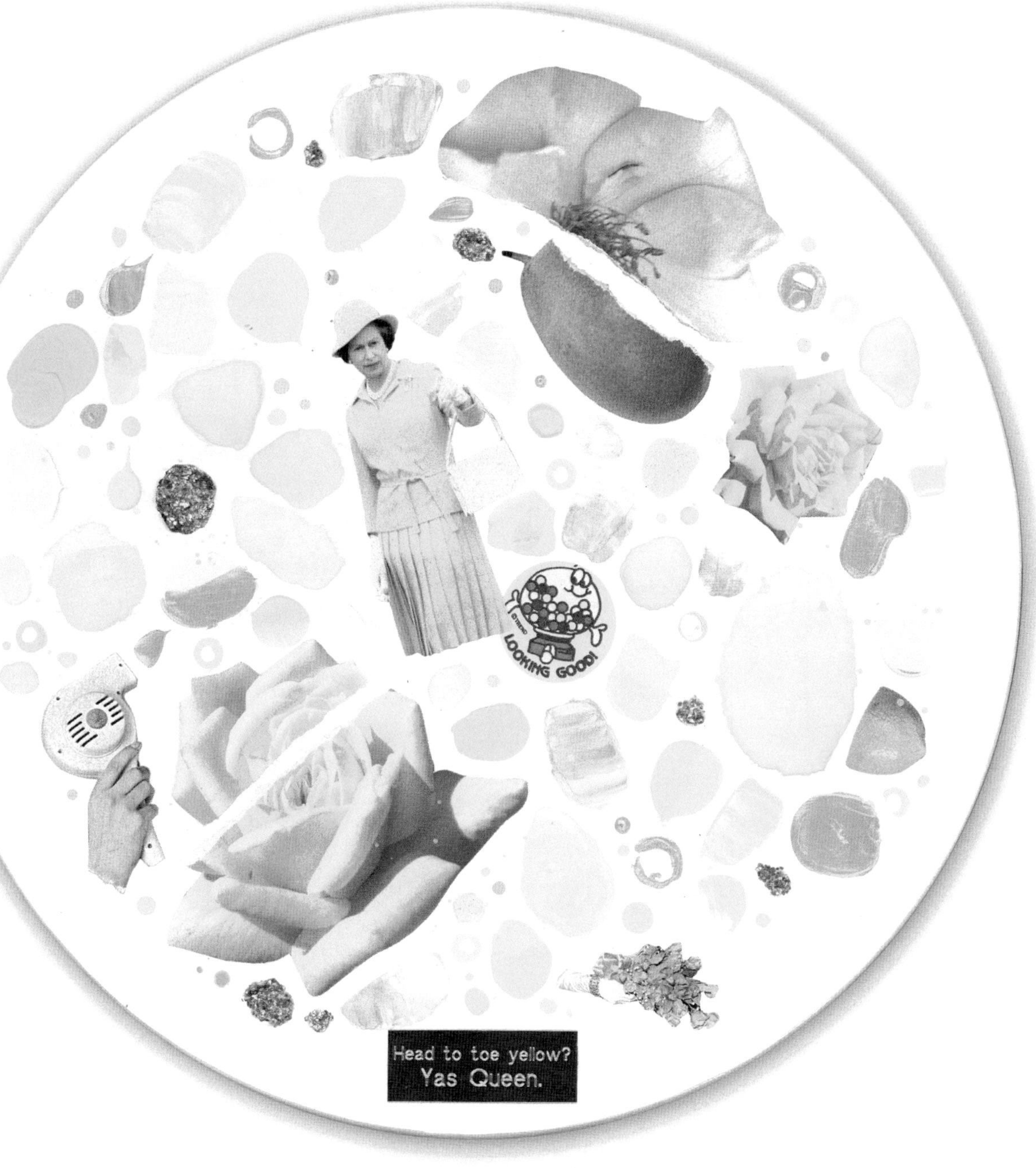

Danielle Krysa, *Head to Toe Yellow? YAS QUEEN*, 2019, Mixed Media, Collage on Panel, Doug + Laurie Kanyer Art Collection

Another way is to place elements on the substrate and move them around for a while, waiting to glue them down. Dr. Steven Rudin, a collagist and retired psychiatrist, does just this. Steven will take up to a year in his collage-making process. He moves elements around, considering what relationship they have with the other elements in the collage. He then ponders what thoughts or memories they bring forth for him. In his collage-making process, he is thoughtfully mining his memories while suspending judgement, enlisting the tool of curiosity to consider his reactions and feelings about the arrangement. He does so with reverence and self-respect. Eventually a story or memory may emerge, but he takes his time allowing for the fluidity of memory to come forth and new insights to flow. Refer to the Resource section at the end of the book to learn more about Steven's work and his workshops.

You too can choose to cut out an abundance of elements, move them around, add more, pause for days, and then return to observe the relationship between the elements with curiosity, considering what they stir in you. You can choose to approach this process with self-compassion and acceptance. You can enjoy the creative process of just observing, reflecting, and pondering, while reveling in the new awareness you have developed about yourself and your world.

GEM 10 ▷ **Collage Helps to Illustrate Your Song**

Deep in your heart you carry your song, your very own rhythm and lyric. It came with you at your birth. Your song consists of the noises you heard from the womb and the beating of your mother's heart. It encapsulates your True Self—the desire, passion and purpose of the one and only you. You and your song are united. The beating of your heart coincides with the rhythm of your song as you wake and walk, and as you lay down and sleep.

You have known it from the beginning and yet you have likely forgotten it. Some say our mothers give us our song and our fathers show us how to live it. In the best of circumstances our mothers were curious to hear our song and would listen for the notes beyond our cries for support. Our fathers, once hearing the song, would treasure it and nurture it to be sung. They would support it in the process of entering the world to join all of the other songs.

Sadly, the song often gets stifled or even silenced, but it is always there. It is available to us to set the pace for our lives and to combat criticism, rejection, and hardship. It is there to reject the negative self-talk most of us develop that sets the path of our thinking. Your song plays constantly, but its volume can be turned down with the pressure of the untruths and burdens of life. In its original state it would be so loud that nothing could penetrate it. This is why we crave music and why we find it to be healing. It helps us to recall our own song, and stirs us to find it.

Collage can help you to SEE your song. Your first language is sight. You heard your song in the womb, and once you were born you came to know your world through vision. Seeing, for humans, is believing. So, what if you started to discover your song by making collages about the loves of your life, the things that comprise the notes of your very own song? What if rather than waiting for someone to write a song for you, you collage the elements that comprise the musical score of your song?

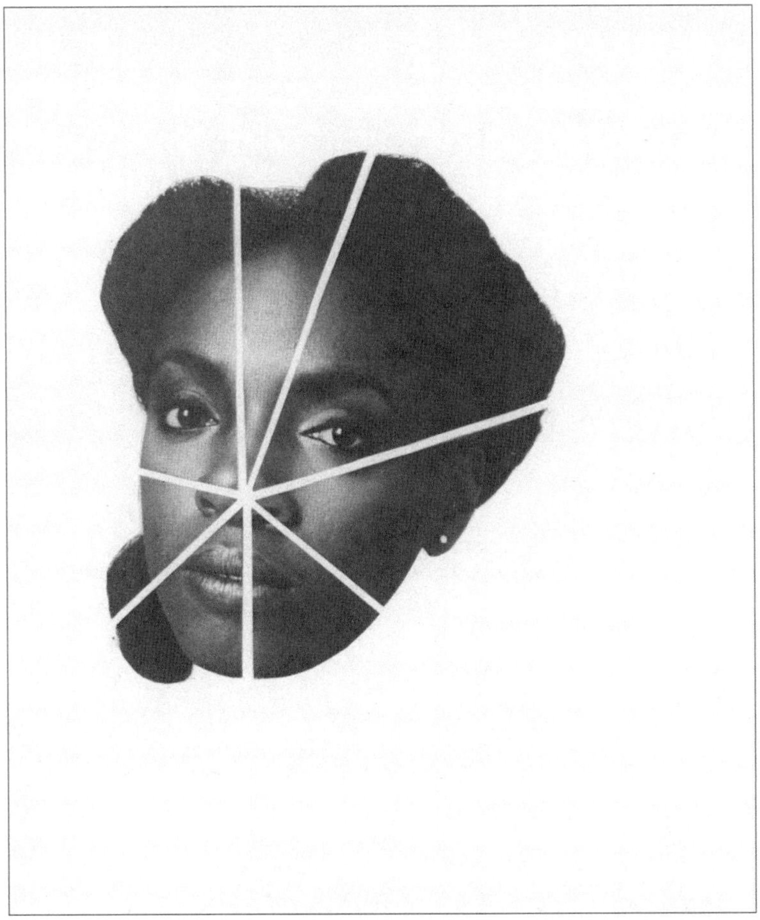

Alexandria Valentine, *Black and Blue*, 2020, Collage, Doug + Laurie Kanyer Art Collection

Cecil Touchon, *Fusion Series 3287*, 2012, Collage, Doug + Laurie Kanyer Art Collection

Erin Houghtaling, *Untitled*, 2020, Collage, Doug + Laurie Kanyer Art Collection

Gems Supporting Feelings

"Every human being is an artist, a freedom being,
called to participate in transforming and
reshaping the conditions, thinking
and structures that shape
and inform our
lives."

—Joseph Beuyers

GEM 11 ▷ **Collage Facilitates the Process of Transforming Feelings**

To transform your emotions using collage, it may be helpful to know each of the individual steps in the process of expressing feelings.

A healthy and ideal expression of feelings can be like taking steps on a staircase. As you go through your day, events take place and some bring forth emotions. Some of the situations elicit a small reaction that you barely notice. Others may bring a more pronounced, strong emotional response. In these heavier times, you have a chance to process the emotions, the related feelings, and transform them to assist you in managing the circumstances.

Below you will find the steps you take on what I refer to as the Feeling Staircase™, a model for processing emotions. Collage can be used as a tool to help you take each step up the staircase. The Gems in the this chapter further discuss these steps and other ideas about transforming feelings.

Stair One: An event takes place, then you have an emotional response that registers in your body and you formulate a primary feeling or a series of feelings.

Stair Two: Ideally, you give yourself permission to feel and express your feeling(s) to yourself or someone else.

Stair Three: You notice your feeling(s) and consider what you are saying to yourself and becoming aware of what is happening in your body, signaling you to pay attention.

Stair Four: You access your feeling(s) by deciphering the source of the feelings at the same time considering what caused this flood of feelings and reflecting on the event more deeply.

Stair Five: You label your feeling(s) with word(s), phrase(s), or collage(s) to accurately identify your feelings. See page #226 for an abundant list of feeling words. Notice the variety and intensity of the words and how each possesses a nuanced meaning.

Stair Six: You express your feeling(s) by making a collage and talking to someone including yourself.

Stair Seven: You witness yourself expressing the feeling(s). This means, for the purpose of this book, actually seeing yourself making the collages.

Stair Eight: You accept and validate your feelings.

Stair Nine: You pace, modulate, and regulate your emotions by the active process of using collage.

Stair Ten: You use the feeling(s) as a signal to inform decision-making. Yes, you can think and feel at the same time!

Stair Eleven: You consider your choices; such as gathering more information, asking for suggestions from others, or pausing for a time.

Stair Twelve: You move forward by either activating a choice(s) or letting the situation go—having now expressed your feelings.

Knowing the steps of the Feeling Staircase gives you deeper knowledge about what you go through when experiencing an emotion and how to transform your feelings to use them as helpers to support your wellness and resolve your concerns.

Betty Klaasse, *Portal - I'll Take Your Brain To Another Dimension*, 2020, Collage Print, Doug + Laurie Kanyer Art Collection

GEM 12 ▷ **Collage Paces Stress Hormones**

When you experience a significant strain or an event that causes you stress, the brain secretes powerful hormones called cortisol and adrenaline throughout the body (Kanyer, 2004). These hormones are there to signal and equip your entire system to address something vital to pay attention to, often a perceived or real threat. Cortisol is known as the stress hormone. It is associated with keeping the body on high alert and poised to respond. Adrenaline causes your heart rate to accelerate and your hands to sweat in anticipation of the need to act in order to remain safe. This is your fight, flight, or freeze response. Your brain will release both of these potent hormones in response to a critical situation.

Prolonged exposure to cortisol and adrenaline can negatively impact the entire body and emotional status. But the simple, repetitive acts involved in building a collage may help reduce the harmful effects of these chemicals. When you are making a collage, especially while cutting out the elements or simply turning the pages, you are using the small muscles of the hands in repetitive motions. This has a calming, meditative effect. It helps to pace the heavy stress hormones releasing from the brain, reducing strain and stress throughout your entire body, while increasing your comfort and well-being.

GEM 13 ▷ **Collage Helps Work Through Mental Blocks and Emotional Loops**

There are times when one's creativity can be paused in a mental block for an unknown reason. There are also times when you find yourself on an emotional merry go round, looping on a particulate emotional tone. Both mental blocks and emotional loops can can feel stagnating and sluggish. While different, they are essentially about being stuck. Most people in these heavier times want to move forward and get on with life. This can add even more strain on one's system.

There are numerous reasons mental blocks and emotion loops can happen. Surprisingly they often take place just before a big developmental leap of emotional awareness or a creative break through. So take heart! Other times there are issues that need to be released and some new insight is required. Occasionally, the issues are related to others and you may be absorbing their load.

No matter the cause, the brain is so remarkable that it can detect a problem and then work to solve or right the concern. The brain knows things are not on track. This can cause racing internal pressure to surge forward. It can be like stacking blocks, each one adding more weight, with the chance of a big tumble. You don't have to be crippled by these times of being stuck in the mud. A tool like collage can help.

When facing emotional loops or mental blocks it is key to not overextend yourself, whereby placing undue pressure to perform or change. It is wise to invest in smaller tasks that are interesting and calming, while recalling times when you found your way out of the mud.

Consider gathering some source material and cutting out an abundance of words, say well over 100. The act of cutting alone will be soothing. Now find a container and place all the words inside. Try pulling five words from the container and make a small poem. Don't worry if it does not make sense. Once you find a combination of words that you like, make a collage about the subject of the poem. Take one word and look up the definition. From there explore and research the word to learn something new. Make a collage out of what you discover. You could also choose just one word and think of a time from your life the word brings to mind. Make a collage about what you recall and see where that leads you.

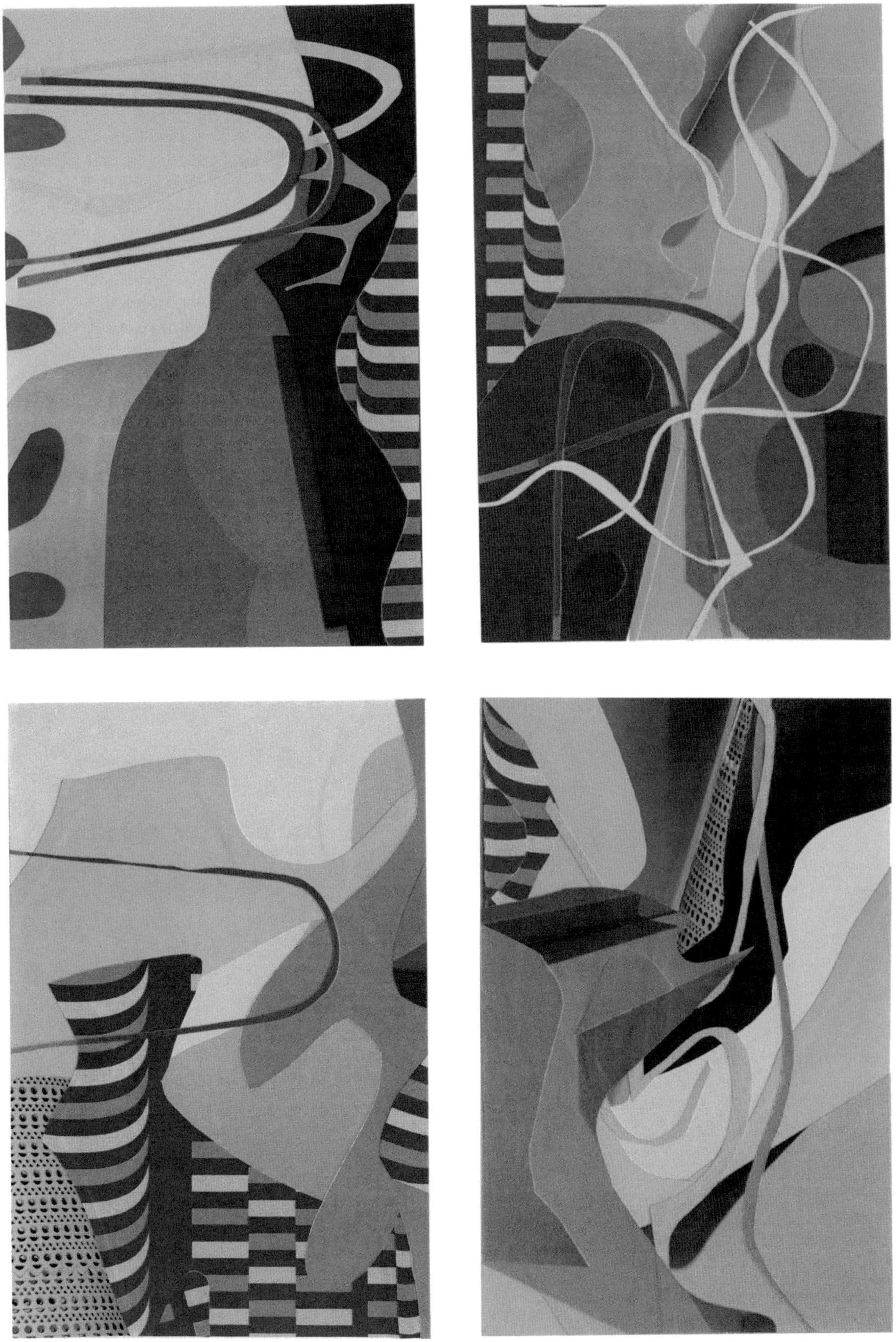

Steven Rudin, *Back to Basics*, 2020, Collage, Doug + Laurie Kanyer Art Collection

Times of emotional loops or mental blocks are like what takes place for the lily flower. Prior to becoming the brilliant specimen, rising above the waters edge, it incubated in the deep, dark mud, gathering strength to emerge into its full majesty. The lily, not having the brain of a human, does not fret in the time of darkness. No, for its very survival it embraces the darkness and sees it as part of the necessary steps in its life span. Don't be fooled, the lily is most definitely moving forward, but at a different pace than when it stretches to meet the sun. As you make collages during a time of emotional loops and or mental blocks, you are not stuck in the mud, you are contributing to your new phase in personal development. Take heart, make a collage!

GEM 14 ▷ **Collage Confronts and Shields from Shame**

Shame is used to control and undermine people. It is different from guilt, where you may have done something and you need to make amends. Shame uses schemes to make people feel worthless, statements like "you're a failure as a person, you are bad to the core, you are completely inadequate" are often used to undermine self-esteem. In her book, *Life Beyond Shame: Rewriting the Rules*, therapist Connie Dawson says "Shame dims our original light. It is a colorless shroud that covers our eyes and holds us back from seeing what we see and knowing what we know. It is a murky layer that has a way of binding us up and keeping us from becoming the person we are meant to be" (Dawson 2016). Dawson identified rules used to keep others in a state of shame (Dawson 2016).

Rule One - Be perfect.
Rule Two - Blame.
Rule Three - Do not feel, ignore feelings.
Rule Four - Keep secrets, tell lies and do not tell.
Rule Five - Be unclear and unaccountable.
Rule Six - Be in control.

Collage is a brilliant way to confront any shame in your life. Make a collage for each of the rules you experience in your life. Once completed, turn each collage over and write with collage elements accurate and truthful rules about yourself. Use the new rules collage as a shield for any shame others pour out in the future. Author Brene Brown says, "Shame thrives in secrecy, silence, and judgement" (Brown, 2020). It is vital to shed shame by sharing your collages with someone you can trust to dissolve the power it has in your life.

GEM 15 ▷ **Collage Offers Permission to Feel and Express Your Emotions**

To transform your emotions you have to give yourself permission to do so. This means when you have a life event that brings forth an emotion, you give the green light of permission to pay attention and attend to the feelings you are encountering. Permission to feel is vital, as it allows you to make an investment in sorting out what is taking place for you, rather than overriding and ignoring your emotions (Brackett, 2019).

By giving yourself permission, it is not to say you are opening a floodgate to dramatic expression; rather, it is to be able to process what you are coming across as a valuable item to address, untangle, and transform. You are making an investment in your well-being, permitting yourself to listen, respond and react to the event, rather than stifling it, which can lead to an emotional explosion.

Permission to feel holds at its core the philosophy that emotions and feelings are signals to pay attention to and address in a situation; leading to clearer and accurate decision-making (Brackett, 2019). It is common for some to initially have a hard time with the processing of their feelings based on a combination of past experiences, their cultural group's opinions, role stereotyping and other outside conditions. Nonetheless, you can begin to offer yourself permission to sort your feelings out. Making a collage will help.

Kelly Schaub, *Shrouded Behind Facade*, 2018, Collage, Doug + Laurie Kanyer Art Collection

Each time you sit to make a collage, you are offering yourself the opportunity to process the emotions. You are physically giving yourself permission to feel. This commitment to making collage will challenge your earlier beliefs about feelings. As you offer yourself permission to feel and make collages, you will be tending to your psychological well-being and making a contribution to your sense of self-worth in a respectful and honoring manner.

GEM 16 ▷ Collage Allows Observation of the Physical Sensations Connected to Feelings

When a potent event happens, the emotional control center of your brain (your limbic system) activates, setting off a multitude of alerts. Chemicals send signals to your nervous system and body to act. This chemical process can also create an emotion or series of emotions that might help you make meaning of the situation. This physiological and emotional process is a survival experience designed to keep you safe and protected.

You can use collage to help familiarize yourself with this gift of protection in recognizing what your typical body sensations mean. This process can support you in attuning to your body sensations. You can learn to listen to what they are saying to you when facing an important event. You can make a collage that documents the physical sensations you notice during a potent event.

In making your collage, you can reflect on past or present potent events and recall or record your physical sensations/actions. Were you wringing your hands, clenching your jaw, tapping your feet, feeling heat in your chest? What does your body do when experiencing potent feelings?

Recording this on a collage and getting to know yourself better will then help you the next time you are faced with these types of sensations. You will recognize the physical signs earlier and be able to use them to help you. You can deepen your knowledge of these signals to transform a situation. As you do, your physical signals can become honored friends, alerting you to solve a concern, have an important conversion, write a clarifying email, or something else, all in efforts to improve the quality of your life. Having awareness and paying attention to your physical sensations will allow you to then use methods (such as attending to your breath) to de-escalate and reduce the strain on your system.

GEM 17 ▷ Collage Expands Your Vocabulary of Feeling Words

Imagine viewing the most incredible color on the feathers of a bird. The color is new to you and it is exquisite—truly remarkable. However, you don't seem to have the words to describe the profound color right in front of you. You have no way to know how to label the color, no accurate word comes to mind. This would be incredibly stifling and frustrating.

This happens all the time for people as they work to express their feelings. Your vocabulary of feeling-words is initially developed in early childhood, as others give you the words for what they think you are feeling. You go on from there to create your own personal dictionary of feeling-words to use over time. Like the situation above, you may need to expand your collection of words to share what you are feeling.

The vocabulary of words you use to express feelings can expand at any time in your life. Being able to accurately label the way you are feeling about an event or situation is vital to well-being, self-confidence, and connection with others. As you make collages, you are inundated with words on the pages of your source materials. Writers go out of their way to find exceptionally descriptive words to tell their story. In making collage you are exposed to an abundance of words, which you can adopt and use to express your feelings.

Bill Noir, *Floral Thought*, 2015, Collage, Doug + Laurie Kanyer Art Collection photo

You do not have to stay stifled with a limited vocabulary when you make collages. You can collage as a way to intentionally build a more extensive personal dictionary of feeling-words. In fact, you can choose to make a collage of only feeling-words to help to remind you.

Please refer to page 226 for a list of feeling words to expand your vocabulary.

GEM 18 ▷ **Collage Validates and Acknowledges Feelings**

The process of tending to your emotions is enhanced when you and others validate and acknowledge what you are feeling. To be able to share your feelings and have another person listen—nodding their head, letting you know they hear what you are telling them—is life-giving.

Most often as you tell others about what you feel, they will actually mirror back to you the facial expression you are making. In doing so, they are showing you how you are feeling and this validates you. It can be heavy to experience something challenging without another person's verbal and non-verbal validation. To have others validate your feelings helps you to feel accepted and shows others care.

As you search through your source materials for elements to build your collage, you will see faces of people expressing different emotions in relation to things in life. Seeing what others are feeling in the source material is as if they are reflecting back to you what you are feeling. In a remarkable way, the images are like a mirror to you, validating your feelings. It is as if you have told them your story and they show you on their faces a reflection of what you are experiencing—what you are feeling. This causes you to feel heard and understood, validated and acknowledged. You are not alone with your feelings when making a collage.

Making a collage also validates your feelings by allowing you to recognize that someone else felt what you feel and understands your emotions. Other people have felt exactly what you are feeling. This enables you to have empathy and helps to foster a deeper, more compassionate connection with yourself and others.

GEM 19 ▷ **Collage Offers Visual Cues**

There are times when you may not know exactly how you feel. While looking for elements to make your collage, you find an array of descriptive expressions on the faces of people in the source materials. These visual cues will help you to define what you are feeling. Sometimes a situation emerges that is new and you haven't developed a typical feeling response. Maybe the situation is so confounding that you struggle to put your finger on what you're feeling.

Moments like these can hinder your ability to express your emotions and thoughts because you flounder for some time without knowing what to do and how to feel. It is as though you are frozen in place, stuck in a space of unknowing. This happens to all of us from time to time, and it can be very confusing and frustrating. Making a collage will give you insight by offering visual cues on how to respond by seeing the vast variety of people's response on the pages of your source materials.

It is important to understand that as we grow up we learn from others about feelings within a cultural context. This includes how to express feelings and the words we use to label them. When the cultural groups you're surrounded by have limited vocabulary or patterns of expression, this can also make it difficult to express feelings.

ØjeRum, *Untitled*, 2019, Doug + Laurie Kanyer Art Collection

As you make collage, you will expose yourself to a plethora of images that show faces expressing emotions and this will affirm your feelings, offering you support and affirmation. When faced with a new situation where you have no idea what to feel—having no frame of reference or inherited model for guidance—these visual cues will help support you.

The faces of people in your source material can act as an extended community of sorts, showing you ways people express feelings all over the world and offering you cues to express yours. This will strengthen your ability to express feelings while fortifying your confidence in future, unfamiliar experiences.

GEM 20 ▷ **Collage Communicates Feelings Quickly and Accurately**

Have you ever had the experience of talking in circles? You try to get your point across and it takes multiple conversations that seem to go nowhere. The other person may be truly making an effort to understand your point, but the message may not be fully understood. This is exhausting. It can wear on the relationship and, in many ways, it is a waste of precious time that you will never get back.

In order to feel understood—to feel as though your efforts to communicate are getting across—you need others to mirror, accept, validate, and empathize with what you are feeling and working to express. Accurate communication becomes more challenging when validation does not happen, which is common, especially with the spoken word.

In making a collage, you have the ability to quickly create something to express and gain acceptance for both your feelings and your response to an experience. Collage allows you to gain insight for yourself about the situation, to accept your feelings and gives you the opportunity to assure that your message and emotional reaction are accurate.

From there, you can show it to others so they can see what you are saying. This can encourage further discussion, acceptance, and clarification. It also reduces the time spent struggling to explain your point, as you know what you want to say and the listener has something to visually respond to. Collage will help you clearly communicate your experiences and feelings while enriching the quality of relationships.

GEM 21 ▷ **Collage Confirms Intuition**

Your intuitive process (the internal, often potent impressions nudging you to pay attention to something) comes from one side of your brain (Cherry, 2020). Intuition will often alert and inundate your whole body, mostly your gut, telling you something important is happening. More and more, society is affirming the accuracy of people's intuitive capabilities.

Your logical, language-oriented process, however, comes from another side of the brain (Cherry, 2020). Intuition, the hunch or a gut feeling, is initially unverifiable information, meaning it often comes to you without words. The intuition does not link automatically to the language centers (Cherry, 2020). To decipher your intuition, you need a way to link and employ both of these areas of the brain to confirm and understand your intuitions and act upon them with confidence.

Making a collage offers you a way to coordinate the intuitive and logical areas of the brain, helping to verify your intuition and move to address the situation at hand. In making a collage about what you are intuiting, you are creating an image, giving yourself a visual language to label intuition with words. This offers you a chance to experience your intuition as discernible and real information in a logical manner. Collage makes the invisible world of your intuition visible. It is as if you are able to physically see the energy information in your body appearing on the collage.

Max-o-Matic, *Complexity of Simplicity*, 2017, Collage, Doug + Laurie Kanyer Art Collection

This visual representation will help you to then link the appropriate words in order to share with others what you know. You will then be able to communicate and address the intuited information. Collage will offer you a chance to say with words what you are feeling in order to get help if needed. You will be able to say to a trusted individual, "I had an interesting feeling and I have taken some time to ponder it, and I am able to articulate what it is about. I need some help from you regarding a specific need. Can you help me, or shall I ask someone else?"

Having a visual representation of your intuition (in the form of a collage) will help you clarify the importance and urgency of a key issue. It will help you to hone your intuitive skills as you move from having a hunch to having facts and information. This will help you gain confidence and refine your knowledge and insight.

GEM 22 ▷ **Collage Promotes Letting Go**

There are times when you will find yourself ruminating on events, problems and conversations. You simply can't let go. Placed right at the front of your awareness, they play over and over in your mind and seem to be all-consuming. In times like these, you can make a collage about the situation and it will offer you a chance to reduce and let go of the agitation.

The simple act of cutting and pasting, doing something productive and constructive in the face of irritating concerns, allows the brain to become calmer. Also, when you put the haunting issues troubling your mind into a collage, you get distance from them. They are out of your head and onto the substrate.

In a very real way, you are physically letting go of the thing tumbling around in your mind. This physical distance will allow you to be more objective about the matter—to really analyze if the issue requires this much trouble and energy. You will be able to see what is going on more clearly, and this may stop the issues from continuously rolling around and manipulating your awareness—holding you hostage.

Making a collage will offer a way to reduce the issue's hold on you. This will offer you an opportunity to begin to choose to take more effective action on the matter. Collage is a human event where something powerful shifts, allowing you to let go of things that may have a hold on you.

GEM 23 ▷ **Collage Becomes a Meditation**

Many people make collage as a daily meditative practice. Collage has many of the same benefits of other forms of traditional meditation. In fact, you can do a time of focused breathing first and then begin to collage. When you find a rhythm and routine with making collages daily, it becomes a creative ritual, shaping a pattern to your life and providing stability and predictability. Each day brings so much uncertainty, and it is comforting to have consistent, peaceful time set aside to escape for a moment.

You can approach your daily meditation without an intended goal or you can choose a random word from the dictionary and use it as a theme to make a collage. You might select to make a collage on the theme of something you read that has religious or spiritual subject matter or pick up a volume of Rumi and make a collage about what you read.

Collage can become a daily self-care practice—a meditation, a prayer or time of retreat—offering a quiet space of creative enjoyment. Your collage-making space can be dedicated as a sacred sanctuary space in your home. As you make collage part of your day it will help to regulate, modulate, and transform your emotions and life events, offering you a period of contemplation and reflection. It can also serve as a daily visual record of your life.

Teresa "Tess" Ettel, *Stella*, 2019, Collage, Doug + Laurie Kanyer Kanyer Art Collection

To simplify the process, I suggest you use a triangle, but you might choose another shape—a heart, square, circle—that you place each day on the substrate to start. Then, you might choose a few elements for your collage to describe or define your day so that your daily practice does not become too labor intensive.

Kellette Elliott, a talented collagist and arts educator, makes a collage each day. She is a master of minimalist collages, featuring only a few elements selected with profound contemplation and intention to tell deep and visually powerful stories. You will find you come to look forward to the soothing ritual, and it will provide order for you in an otherwise disorderly world.

GEM 24 ▷ **Collage Safely Releases Angry Feelings**

There are times in your life where you might feel so strongly that your anger becomes melded with passion. This is a potent and explosive combination, as it hijacks clear thinking without a way to manage yourself. This combination of anger and passion may cause you to behave in ways you would have never imagined.

Unchecked, your anger/passion feeling not only leaves a chance for lashing out at others with harmful outcomes, it also risks impacting your entire system. Let me say that tending to your emotions and feelings on a regular basis will decrease the chance of this type of response. This is one of the many reasons why making a collage regularly is a good practice for self-care.

Unexpressed emotions can quickly add up to an explosive outburst. When you feel that potent combination, knowing you clearly should not act on it, you can safely release the emotion and get it out through the process of making a collage. Obviously, it is best to tear the paper rather than use scissors or other sharp instruments when you're extremely angry. This type of collage is like stepping into a fuss box of sorts. Since the source material isn't precious, it can be destroyed or cut up to make something else.

This can be a cathartic destruction of these potent reactions, cleansing you of their impact, allowing for better analysis of the situation. And, once your feelings shift (and they will) take a moment and find an element to represent a choice you will make about the situation.

GEM 25 ▷ **Collage Offers a Focal Point**

One of the most effective ways to find balance when facing strain is to ground yourself by finding a visual focal point. Understand that the mind, when in a stressful state, can often lead you down a treacherous road, revisiting past hardships you've experienced in life. Or the mind can begin to take memories from the past and project fears of those events into the future with unfounded notions of destruction. This projection takes place because memories can be clearly linked to the network of the mind. The fight, flight, and freeze hormones are alerted and, before you know it, you are in a tailspin of uncertainty. You are plagued with the "what was" or the "what ifs."

Making a collage is an excellent way to find or make a visual focal point to ground yourself. In this circumstance, I suggest a special collage that I call a Centering Collage™. A Centering Collage is one where you focus on what you see right in front of you, observing and accounting for the objects of the environment you are in. You then make a collage about what you see, be it a chair in the corner amidst a flurry of dirty clothes or your cup of steaming hot coffee against the clouds through a window. Once it is made, you can keep your collage visible in your immediate environment. It becomes a calming focal point, a place to visit when you feel the pull of the "what was" and the "what ifs."

Twiggy Boyer, *Finding a Place of My Own*, 2019, Collage, Doug + Laurie Kanyer Art Collection

As you practice this skill of grounding yourself, it will enhance positive character traits. You will forge new neural pathways—roads in your mind of patience and strength. Then you can reflect on the collage you made that will remind you of your positive character traits—your efforts to thrive—and bring you back to a time of comfort. It will give you a focal point, helping you to stay in the present, rather than the slippery slope of the past or the future.

GEM 26 ▷ **Collage Allows for Dramatic Expression When You Just Have to Scream**

We all experience moments of anxious frustration—when you just want to scream. Starting in childhood, the need to have a tantrum (a big feeling) may persist throughout our lifetime. But the urge to let out a primal howl seems to only fuel the intensity you feel inside and holding it back can make it worse.

Naturally, there is a balance between letting out a solid scream and holding it in. There is great benefit in what is called mirroring, where one person mirrors the sentiment of another with the same exact affect. You see this in sporting events where a team of players will howl together in frustration or celebration. The mirroring recharges, affirms, validates, and helps them to move on to address what is causing a dramatic response.

Imagine how much more heard you would feel if you had a collage of a screaming person. When you make a collage of someone screaming, you can affirm your feelings and even decrease your anxiety. You can then view your collage, and it will validate how you feel, allowing you to safely release these potent feelings before you start screaming yourself! The process will give you calming relief by affirming your feelings and that very human urge to scream.

GEM 27 ▷ **Collage Values Mess-Making**

Life and emotions can feel messy. When making collages, you will make a mess—it is inevitable. There are deep psychological benefits to the messes that come with making a collage. Seeing the mess can visually affirm what you are going through. In observing the large and small fragments of your cutting scraps, you also see the large and small aspects of your real life mess that may need to be addressed.

You might think experiencing a messy life situation and being surrounded by the mess of your collage-making would just add more stress. In actuality, when going through a messy life experience, it can be comforting to have a visual symbol of the circumstances. In most cases, the collage mess is not overflowing to the entire house; rather, it is contained to a small, designated area. This shows that the world is much larger than the mess you face in front of you. You can walk away from the collage mess from time to time, take a break and return to work on it later. You can learn to momentarily park even the most consuming of messy events.

Moreover, you can make a collage from these scraps to illustrate that messes can actually lead to something good; that positive things can arise from bad situations. When it comes time to clean up the mess, you will demonstrate your self-efficacy in doing so and find comfort in seeing that the other mess in life will eventually pass.

GEM 28 ▷ **Collage Practices the Art of Flow to Ease Stress**

When you experience some perceived strain—the type that might frighten you or cause you to be on high alert—the part of your brain that ignites the fight, flight, or freeze response can get activated. When faced with a real threat this response is designed to help you to achieve safety from harm. It is a helpful response left over from our primal days, our early human beginnings, to help us survive.

Jake Kennedy, *Pink Shaft*, 2019, Collage, Doug + Laurie Kanyer Art Collection

Depending on your past experiences this response may be very close to the surface and readily available. The fight, flight or freeze response is often triggered by a sensory experience. A simple smell can remind you of a past wound that can cause you to move into fight, flight, or freeze.

There is an alternative I call flow. In many cases the brain is on autopilot when it moves into fight, flight, or freeze and misreads the situation. Flow is a better response, as most of us are not being chased by a tiger wanting to eat us as our caveman ancestors experienced. Flow offers replacement to the other alternatives and has a restorative effect; rather than the destructive effect of getting into a fight, running away, or freezing which allows others to take advantage. The fight, flight, or freeze response often carries the hormones of adrenaline and cortisol through the body, which can be harmful over time.

To move into flow the first thing to do is breathe. This will signal to the brain you are alive and in no harm. The second thing to do is lower your shoulders. Now connect with your heart and soul centers by placing one hand on your chest and the other on your abdomen. Breathe in and out deeply for as many minutes as you need to quiet yourself. Close your eyes and see yourself flowing in the air, water, or somewhere comfortable.

Once you have settled into flow, move to making a collage with elements showing a calm, settled, safe, and comfortable tone. As you cut the collage elements breathe in, significantly slowing down your cutting process, taking your time to sink into the safety of your surroundings. You can tear the paper out too, doing so in a paced and tranquil fashion. As you apply glue, do so like you might be frosting a cupcake. Swirl the glue and let it flow onto each of the elements. When you apply each element to the substrate, swish them around and flow it onto the paper like a glider plane flowing in the sky.

In making a flow collage you are offering your mental system a new memory experience to compare and to choose from when facing a perceived threat. Each time you find yourself feeling the old familiar fight, flight, or freeze response, choose to use flow instead and enjoy the benefits.

GEM 29 ▷ **Collage Shows What is Under the Surface**

When you are having an emotional response to something, you display some aspects of the feelings to yourself and others. There is often more going on inside of you than meets the eye. It is in some ways like an iceberg on the ocean. You see the tip of the iceberg, but below the surface of the water is much more (Johnston, 1984).

As you build a collage about what you are experiencing and explore related feelings, you will be able to mine other aspects of the situation—to see the rest of the iceberg. Chunks of the iceberg, other aspects of your feelings hidden below the water, will loosen as you collage. They will rise to the surface of the water, your conscious awareness, for you to consider and ponder.

You can then search for and discover elements to portray those chunks of emotional icy weight floating on the surface of your conscious awareness. As you do so, you might begin to reflect on how to manage this deeper understanding. Once these chunks are represented in collage, you can begin to examine them, one at a time. In doing so, you are able to navigate the situation with greater awareness and self-compassion. You will, in making collage, know more about the impact an event or life circumstance has on you.

Lara Rouse, *The Kennedys*, 2019, Collage, Doug + Laurie Kanyer Art Collection

Aaron Beebe, *Zag*, 2020, Collage, Doug and Laurie Kanyer Art Collection

Gems Reducing Stress

"Remember that stress doesn't come from what's
going on in your life. It comes from
your thoughts about what's
going on in your life"

—Andrew Bernstein

GEM 30 ▷ **Collage Exercises Areas of the Brain—Releases Positive Hormones**

Collage helps to motivate the pleasure centers of the brain to release happy hormones. One such hormone, dopamine, is often associated with the anticipation of happiness, pleasure, and achieving a goal. When you anticipate the collage-making experience, your brain will release dopamine into the body, which can increase pleasure, attention, mood, and motivation (Kanyer, 2018). The brain also releases endorphins when making collage (Kanyer, 2018). Endorphins are known to decrease pain and stress, helping you to persevere in trying circumstances. The excretion of these hormones will rejuvenate your entire body as you make a collage, putting you into a feel-good state (Otto, 2016).

GEM 31 ▷ **Collage Releases Pressure by Emptying Your Brain**

You can make a collage about all the ideas, pressures, strains, and joys you have stored in your brain. You may often find that you have so much going on—many details and events—that you need to set them outside of your brain. You can place them all in a collage, allowing for visual order and clarity of the various things rolling around in your head. From there, you can better decide what to address first. Too often, a to-do list only causes more stress. A collage brain dump, where you find elements for all the things on your mind and place each on the collage, offers an easy way to examine all the details so you can begin to process and prioritize what needs to be done and what can be set aside.

GEM 32 ▷ **While Choosing Elements Collage Calms the Body**

Making a collage often involves cutting items out of a magazine or a book. The act of cutting elements out actually supports healing of emotional strain, stress, and anxiety. By using the small muscles of the hands in a repetitive motion, you support the pacing or movement of stress hormones through the body (Kanyer 2004).

The simple act of cutting or even tearing paper helps to regulate, settle, and modulate the potency of emotional strain. The repetitive motion, both rhythmic and meditative, calms and soothes the nerves and helps to ground you, improving your emotional well-being. Like knitting or going for a walk, making collage is a wonderful way for you to relax, let go of life strains, and have some fun (Kanyer 2004).

Consider focusing on cutting out a single-themed item. An example would be birds. Searching for single themed elements will use the small muscles of your hand to turn the pages, and focusing on a single subject will set a meditative tone for a time. Find a file or envelope to store the collection of birds. When you want to use a bird in a collage, you'll have it all ready to go. You will delight in your own cleverness and planning when it comes time to use a bird in a collage. You might know the feeling of contentment when you go to find a tool you need and can locate it with ease. The confidence and ease of strain can really be an emotional boost. When you go to your file and find a bird, it is just like a little wink to enhance your self-esteem.

GEM 33 ▷ **Collage Offers a Needed Escape**

When you look at source materials to make your collage, you can experience a visual escape far away from your current concerns. You might not be able to go on a long road trip, but looking at a magazine and making a collage can offer you a mental escape by engaging your creative imagination. In your collage-making you may see a new recipe or a movie idea in the magazine, and that can even take you down a road toward a temporary escape. Collage will introduce you to other aspects of the world. Making a collage, you may be transported to another country, another decade, or a different period in history while you search for elements. This will give you a temporary pause, affording relief by lowering stress levels.

Miranda Milward, *Flying*, 2020, Collage, Doug + Laurie Kanyer Art Collection

GEM 34 ▷ **Collage Investigates the Harmful Effects of Advertising**

Making a collage can help you to identify one source of strain you're having—social pressure brought on by advertising. When making a collage, as you search through magazines for elements, you can't help but notice the advertising and the pressures society places on people. You will come across articles, essays, and interviews, creating an opportunity to reflect and consider how advertising can impact your self-esteem and increase a self-critical voice. This part of the process in collage-making is unique in that it allows you to reflect on the things you observe and read as you work.

If your source material is vintage, from many decades back, you will also be exposed to racism and sexism prevalent in older magazines. For women, people of color, queer people, or other groups that have survived historical oppression, this may be an opportunity to pause and choose another source material for the sake of self-protection. If you are using these antiquated publications, you will likely see blatant efforts to sex role stereotype people and to discriminate against many groups of people. If this subject matter represents traumatic stress for you, create a collage about your resiliency when facing these systems. This will naturally cause you to deeply consider the pressure you and others have experienced at the hands of advertisers to manipulate.

GEM 35 ▷ **Collage Uses Humor to Support Well-Being**

It has been said that humor is a good antidote to pain and suffering. Some of the best comedies are based on real life hardships. In fact, there is powerful evidence proving stress hormones are reduced when humor is used (Mayo Clinic, 2019). One huge benefit of collage is that it gives you the chance to make really silly, goofy, and funny things.

When experiencing emotional upset, humor offers much-needed relief. Being able to put a man with the head of a cat on the wing of a plane, which is silly and impossible, may offer a bit of comic relief during serious and heavy life experiences. Making a humorous, surreal, or silly collage also shows you can have more than one feeling at a time. You can be experiencing hardship, feeling very frustrated, and still make a collage about your favorite joke and feel delight and joy.

GEM 36 ▷ **Collage Uses Potent Words with Some Distance**

Images are one of collage's greatest tools when it comes to transforming emotions and life experiences. But sometimes a word or two can get the message across better. As you pour through your source material to make your collages, naturally you will see words printed on the pages. You can use these words in your collage as a way to pinpoint your feelings, creating a safe distance to express them.

In some cases, the words you might want and need to use are potent, and they carry some strong social overtones. They may be words you've been told you should never speak out loud or even write. You might also fear that if you actually did write down or say these words, others would see you in a negative light. This is when using printed words in your collage will have great value.

Choosing words will give you permission to use the word that fits best, allowing for distance, as you are not the writer of the word itself. This will help you to expel the potency of the situation and shield you from possible ridicule. You may need to find and cut each letter out to form the word. Keep in mind, as you do, it is as though you are performing word surgery. In the same way a surgeon would cut out, expose, and dispose of a cancerous tumor, you expel the sentiments and the situation. You are liberating yourself while simultaneously uniting with all other people who felt the need to express themselves using that very word.

Emma Anna, *On the Spectrum*, 2020, Collage, Doug + Laurie Kanyer Art Collection

GEM 37 ▷ **Collage Invites a Playful Spirit**

Life is way too serious and heavy. You grow up and you are faced with being a grown up! Boring! No fun! Remember when you were a kid and thought, I can't wait to grow up and do exactly what I want to do. It was as if you imagined adulthood would be fun and games, only to discover it's full of responsibility and challenges. Adulting can be a shock to the system, but it's a fact of life and everyone has to do it eventually. Whatever happened to play? What happened to mud puddles and splashing in the wading pool?

It is never too late to play! Never! I don't care what you've been told, keeping the flame of your inner child burning is serious business when it comes to your well-being. Collage is a perfect instrument for you and your inner child to mindlessly play—especially if you bring in bright-colored crayons and markers!

Typically the materials used in collage are generally inexpensive, if not completely free. Just like those mud pies you made in your backyard growing up, with nothing more than a puddle of rainwater and some dirt you stirred with a stick, you don't have to fret about waste or expense.

Collage is perfect for play and exploration, offering you an easy way that allows for abundant discoveries and sheer joy. Collage frees you from the worry and pressure of making a masterpiece. You can cut, tear, and paste while dancing, or just throw the scraps of paper up in the air for that matter! The truth is you need to be goofy as an adult to survive the strain of life and to be at ease through joyful play. Collage play allows for creative expression that can reset your feelings and shift your mood. So get a comic book and cut to your heart's content. Set a timer for 15 minutes of joyful collaging and stay in touch with your inner child.

GEM 38 ▷ **Collage Keeps You From Feeling Overwhelmed**

The cumulative effects of daily life expectations—coupled with a multitude of new concerns, along with the constant bombardment of your internal dialogue—can make it hard to make sense and compartmentalize what is upsetting you. It is as if the emotional response you are having is expanding and growing, getting more complicated, taking on a life of its own. When this happens, it is as if the memories of past pain and suffering, every hurt and wound you experienced, boils up to the brim of your present awareness. Your emotions are like a snowball effect, the initial concern is attached to other pressures and then, in the heat of the situation, you access the depths of your memory and it all gets packed together. You feel as though you could explode.

In times like this—where there is a magnitude of concerns, responsibilities, and pressures piling up in an avalanche of an emotional response—making a collage gives you a place to visually deposit all your thoughts, feelings, and experiences, allowing for a more objective and clear consideration. You need a way to calm the tendencies for your emotions to expand and dip into the past, while handling what you need to address in the present. Collage will also help you to discover and highlight what the trigger for the emotional avalanche was. This will help you to be aware of that hotspot's potency in the future. When you see your completed collage, it gives you an image to affirm your experience and it halts your internal dialogue from magnifying the situation. This will reduce stress, as the feelings of being overwhelmed are replaced with a sense of being in control, fortifying your self-efficacy.

Gherdai Hassell, *Touchstone to be Measured*, 2020, Doug + Laurie Kanyer Art Collection

GEM 39 ▷ **Collage Offers Quick Revision—Encourages Change and Life Improvement**

You may feel like you are often stuck in a rut and can't seem to make even the smallest of shifts. In making a collage, you can gain insight into what is causing you to spin your wheels and reveal possibilities in other areas of your life. With collage, you can make quick, easy revisions just by cutting, tearing, and rearranging the elements, inspiring change and helping to make shifts.

The very nature of creating a collage is easy-breezy and helps decrease anxiety caused by the ever-present fear of making a mistake, freeing you to connect and respond to your intuition. When making a collage you can experience creative problem solving quickly and see new opportunties throughout the process. You are reminded that you can make moves toward change—that things will improve—and your life circumstances will benefit because of it. This will support your self-efficacy and increase your feeling of personal power.

Carlotta Speroni, *Inner peace - Dreaming of wider spaces*, 2020. Collage, Doug + Laurie Kanyer Art Collection

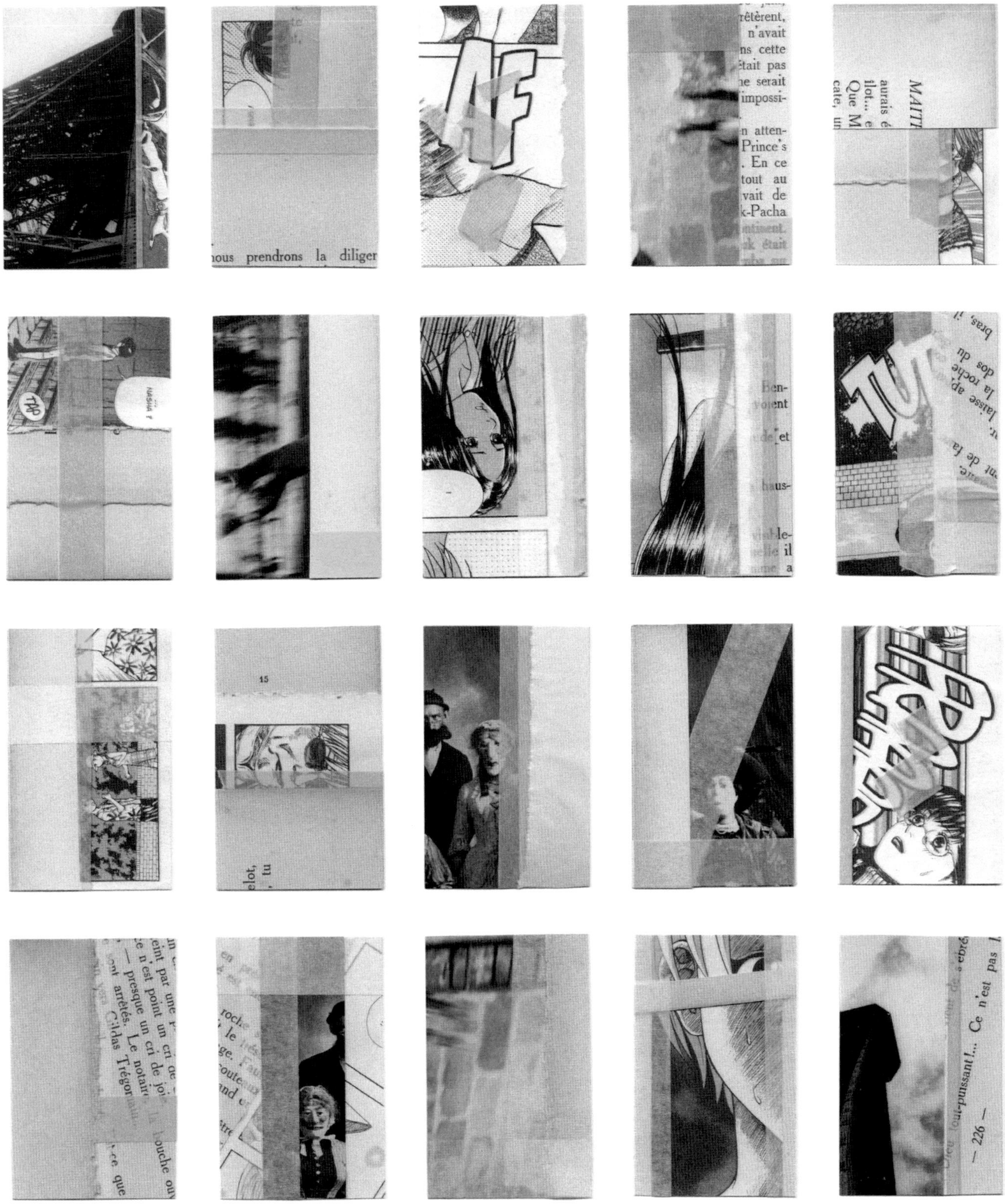

Petra Zehner, *Finding Joy in the Smallest of Things*, Twenty Mini Collages, Doug + Laurie Kanyer Art Colletion

Carol White, *Woman with Owls*, 2019, Collage, Doug and Laurie Kanyer Art Collection

Gems Affirming Self Awareness & Identity

"The unexamined life is not worth living."

—Socrates

GEM 40 ▷ **Collage Deepens Self-Awareness and Offers Access to Your True Self**

When you are creating a collage, you are also tapping into the depths of your subconscious. You have an opportunity to access and know your True Self. During this process, you may notice things of which you weren't initially aware, but your subconscious and True Self find their way into your collages, shining a light on your deeper feelings and your wise insights.

Your True Self is your original divine being, your singular essence, your unique spirit, which first arrived at your birth. Described as 'essence' by authors Don Richard Riso and Russ Hudson in their book, *The Wisdom of the Enneagram; The Complete Guide to Psychological and Spiritual Growth of the Nine Personality Types*, the True Self is often protected by the adapted personality, which develops as we go through life (Hudson, R. and Riso, D.R., 1999).

People often fall asleep, losing contact with their True Self, as they grow and develop their personality and defense mechanisms. They become consumed with the expectations of life, and work at projecting an image designed to protect themselves from pain.

With collage, you bypass the running dialogue of voices in your head—your defense mechanisms and adapted personality—which strive to influence your thoughts about yourself, others, and your experiences. You will be able to park the demands of your day and the influence of your personality to transform your awareness and become reacquainted with your True Self.

GEM 41 ▷ **Collage Echoes Your True Self**

The collages you create can embody and echo your True Self. As you tap into your subconscious during the creative process, your True Self imprints upon, or marries with the materials. This is a true miracle, whereby your soul—your True Self—comes into view in the collage, allowing you to make a mark in this world in a profound manner. It is as though the energy of your very being is being poured into the collage, united with the materials to create a forever stamp, an imprint of your existence and evidence of your True Self.

When you are both the creator and the viewer of the collage, you have the opportunity to see your True Self in a visual way, which will broaden your self-awareness. This process will emerge clearly when you honor the creation without placing any judgment or evaluation on the work, not seeking approval or adulation, merely appreciating it and marveling in what comes forth in the collage.

Moreover, when others view your collage, your True Self echoes from your art and offers the possibility of intermingling with the True Self of the viewer. In some very spiritual way, the viewer becomes more deeply connected to the creator. They have an additional way to know one another. This is truly profound and transformational.

Because each True Self is unique, viewers will respond to art that speaks to their True Self. This is a large part of why you may be drawn to and love certain images, or repelled by and uncomfortable with others. This is also why some art may not resonate with you.

I'm asking you, dear reader, to make a mental leap when considering this; when someone views your collages they have a chance to glimpse your soul. When you view your collages, you are coming into contact with your very being—your True Self. This is truly a phenomenal occurrence. It is precisely the soul work that makes art so important. You and others have a chance to gaze upon your very divine genius!

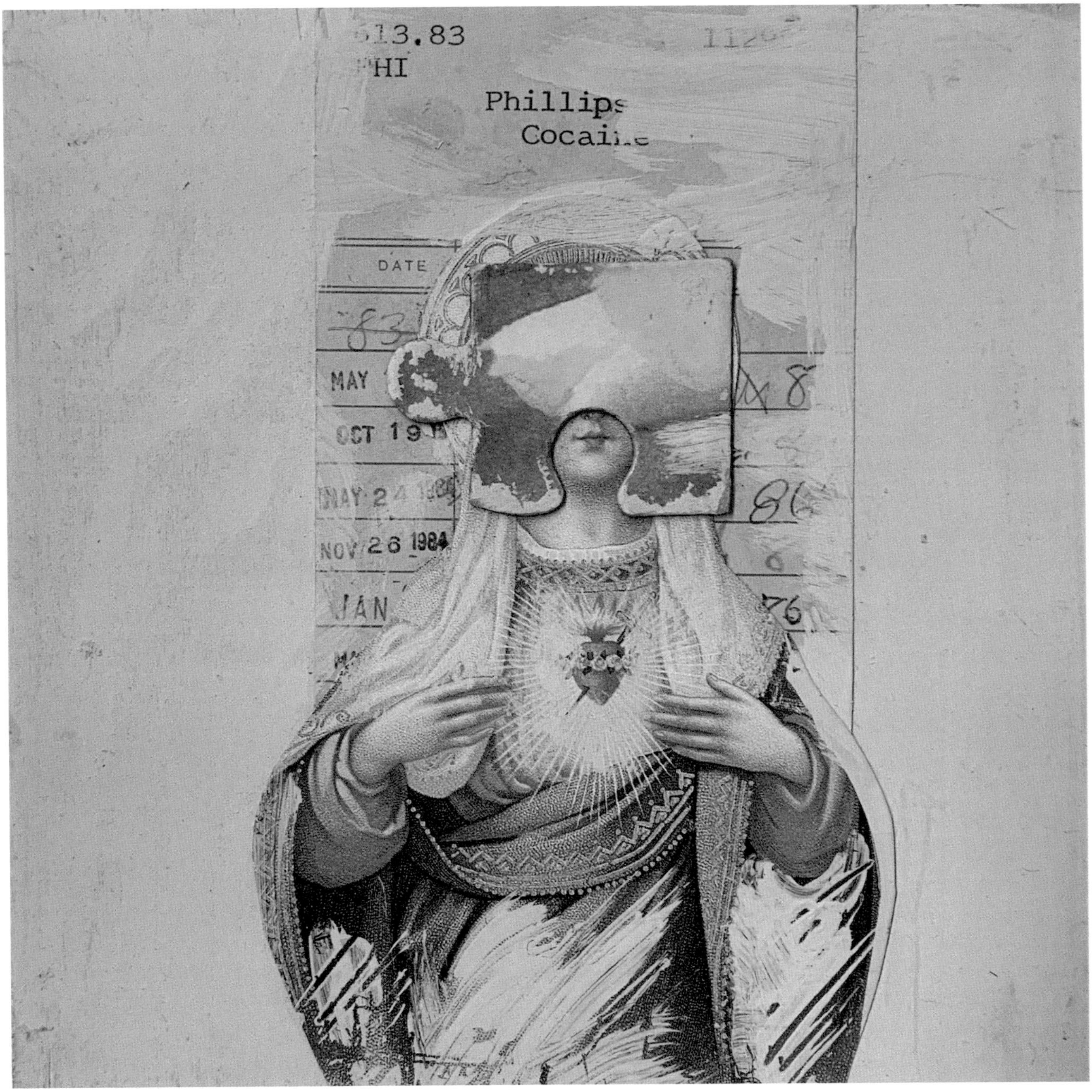

Nancy Kay Turner, *Madonna and Child*, 2018, Collage on Wood, Doug + Laurie Kanyer Art Collection

GEM 42 ▷ **Collage Considers Inherited Stories**

You inherited stories from your family and their past history. These stories likely shaped your identity and became your historical biography. Oral history, the stories of the past expressed verbally from prior generations, was one way groups shape cultural beliefs, values, and set standards for behavior. The stories also served to unite the group and build a tone of belonging. All of these aspects can have a positive influence.

The challenge comes when they provide a limited scope in the expression of emotions, problem-solving, roles, and life choices. Over-identification with the stories you have inherited or the social mores of the group can limit and squash you when you want to go a different way. Poet John O'Donahue wrote, "Your identity is not related to your biography" (Trippet, K., 2008). I would add that experiences you lived or inherited do not define your identity.

To transform your emotions and life events, it is vital you explore the historical stories of your group and their implied expectations. It is key to consider the tales of your ancestors when choosing to adopt their character traits or decide new ones for yourself. There is also value in digging deeper beyond what you were told to see if the stories were complete, honest, and factual—as the teller's memories and recollections have likely shaped the stories.If you have more questions, you might choose to ask others in the group for more information; or, if more realistic and accessible, invest in genealogy services to learn more about your historical ancestry and the related stories.

Collage is a wonderful way to track what your elders have told you, examine how it shaped your self-image, and then literally cut out aspects that do not define you. You can also document on the collage aspects you do identify with and want to expand, replicate, and pass on. You can live beyond inherited family tales from the past to discover your own identity. Choose to collage your own distinctive story.

GEM 43 ▷ **Collage Melts Your Defenses—Reduces the Potency of Your Personality**

As you developed and grew, you may have naturally formed layers of defense mechanisms to protect and shield you from hurt to survive complicated, possibly harmful, life experiences. These defenses are among a number of things that shape your personality and help you to navigate difficulties. Often, though, the defense layers can become too thick and foreboding, closing off the access to your True Self. In other words, to protect yourself, you adopted and formulated a personality you presented to the world. The personality, in some cases, can become so pronounced, so strong, it blocks off parts of yourself, especially your True Self (Hudson, R. and Riso, D.R., 1999).

This idea can be complicated to absorb, so maybe you choose to reflect on the fact that the initial development of defense mechanisms and the resulting personality were formed to help you. Taken too far, the personality can lead to a lack of self-awareness. In a very true way, this means you become separated from your important values, and have limited access to the wisdom of your True Self (Hudson, R. & Riso D. R., 1999).

Making a collage mysteriously helps to ease the grip of the adapted personality so that your defense mechanisms can release and melt a bit. Collage can actually be a way to allow your defenses and personality to let go and move over a bit to offer your True Self a doorway through which it can enter and express itself. This is one of collage's miraculous gifts. It offers you a chance to experience a reduction in your personality's potency that enables you to learn more about who you are at your core.

Martina Pozzi, *1 2 3 stella*, 2020, Collage, Doug + Laurie Kanyer Art Collection

Adam Lalonde, *Finding a Place*, 2020, Collage, Doug + Laurie Kanyer Art Collection

Gems Building Self-Esteem

"Remember always that you not only have the right to be an individual, you have an obligation to be one."

—Eleanor Roosevelt

GEM 44 ▷ **Collage Shows Your Unique Genius**

Each and every one of us has our own unique talents. If every individual in a group were given the exact same elements to make a collage, the outcomes would be uniquely different. All the collages created would be as precious and distinctive as a snowflake or a fingerprint.

Some artists have begun applying this concept to collage. To do so, they start with the same page in a book, or a predetermined single image, and then they all set off to make collages. Eventually, they circle back and show each other the creations. They take joy and delight in all the remarkable, individual uses of the same element. This is an extraordinary tradition of mutually respecting each other's collage creations and relishing in each collagist's individual genius.

If you would like to see an example of this practice, you might refer to Danielle Krysa's book, *Collage: Contemporary Artists Hunt and Gather, Cut and Paste, Mash Up and Transform* (Krysa, 2014). This book beautifully illustrates the practice of a group of artists using a single collage element as a starting point to elevate and celebrate each other's unique genius.

If you want to participate, you can join the weekly collage challenge offered by the Paris Collage Collective (@pariscollagecollective on Instagram), where artist Petra Zehner issues a single element that people all over the world download, print, and make into collages. Once the collages are made, artists post to a designated hashtag on Instagram. Petra then selects a few and highlights them on the Paris Collage Collective Instagram for all to enjoy. Everyone can see the weekly creations by referencing the hashtags #pariscollageclub and #pariscollagecollective. It is phenomenal to observe the unique, creative genius represented in each collage. It is lovely to witness how the world of collage is uplifting and honoring people.

Making collages will give you a way to express your individuality, offering a visual affirmation to demonstrate your singular virtuosity. It will enhance your opinion of yourself as a remarkable soul, worthy of honor and respect. Collage will help you embrace your unique genius and ignite a deeper curiosity toward self-discovery.

GEM 45 ▷ **Collage Helps to Examine & Confront Negative Self-Talk**

You have an internal dialogue called self-talk, a constant back and forth conversation with that little voice in your head. Occasionally, when the mind is under stress, facing challenging circumstances, or even just idly reflecting on things, your self-talk can become harsh or negative, distorting the truth and even lying to you about yourself. In this situation, you are saying things to yourself that are hurtful and untrue.

Sometimes these destructive conversations are based on ill-formed perceptions and conclusions from your past. Other times, it is an endless replay of something hurtful someone said. The causes and origins of negative self-talk vary, yet the words can be destructive to your self-esteem, causing emotional strain.

Due to the negative quality of the thought process in your mind, you could be tearing down your self-esteem. Rather, your self-esteem needs to be about honoring, respecting, and caring for yourself. Making a collage about what you are saying to yourself and about yourself will challenge these thoughts and allow you to analyze the quality of your self-talk while addressing destructive dialogue. As playwright August Wilson said, "Confront the dark parts of yourself, and work to banish them with illumination and forgiveness. Your willingness to wrestle with your demons will cause your angels to sing."

Jesse Freeman, *Inner City Poet*, 2020, Collage Doug + Laurie Kanyer Art Collection

Collage offers a chance to address the distorted thought processes preventing you from honoring and caring for yourself; therefore, helping you move forward in a positive direction. Moreover, the collage will support your efforts to communicate, when consulting a trusted friend on issues of concern, and bring to light a fundamental question—would you talk to anyone else the way you are talking to yourself?

GEM 46 ▷ **Collage Discovers Your True Value**

You may doubt your value and your significance in life. You are not alone in this experience; many people are there too. Somewhere, someone gave you the impression that you are not precious—not of value. This is not true. There are many reasons why this may have happened to you, and it's worth exploring. Making a collage can challenge self-doubt, recalibrate the estimation you hold of your self-worth, and begin to provide you a way to treasure yourself.

When you make a collage, you are using seemingly unimportant, discarded materials—things some would define as valueless or unimportant. As you take the discarded magazine and books, items seen as insignificant, you are elevating them to a new status—one of being worthy to be placed on your collage!

In effect, you are adjusting the definition of the materials from trash to treasure, like a diamond cutter taking a simple, cloudy rock and polishing it into a gemstone. You are redefining the value of the magazines; in doing so, you are actually inviting yourself to see yourself in a different light! As you make collage, you can begin to see the value of these things beyond a negative definition, purpose, and use. This can become true for you, too! We've all heard the expression, one person's trash is another person's treasure. While having a healthy awareness of your ability is wise, you might find an opportunity to challenge the limiting definition you might have of yourself while elevating your self-esteem. As you begin to make collages, you are inviting yourself to see the extraordinary potential of what others might consider useless or junk. This will help you see and appreciate your intrinsic value, beyond what others see, strengthening your self-esteem. You can choose to recycle your life and discard the faulty definition of your true value anytime you want, and collage can help.

GEM 47 ▷ **Collage Confronts Social Conditioning, Peer Pressure, Advertising & Social Media**

While we all want to fit in with our social group and community, the overall social conditioning involving rules, attitudes, and behavioral expectations can squash your soul. You are designed as a unique being, and although acceptance and affirmation are important aspects of belonging, you also need recognition of your distinctive nature. The need to be your unique self, along with the need to belong and the pressures to conform, create a major paradox, causing tension for us all. Making a collage about these social conditioning requirements, or the peer pressures of your group, can help you to decipher what is best for you.

Advertising and social media can also be considered social groups, and they contribute just as much to your feelings of acceptance and belonging. As you make collages, you will be able to address the pressures imposed upon you by advertising and social media, noticing how they affect the way you feel about yourself. You will gain a better perspective on the marketing machine designed to trigger your emotions in order to manipulate your ideas and behavior.

Collage can help you explore and evaluate these pressures. You may choose to deepen your association with them or revise them. In doing so, this will help you to cherish and honor yourself and decipher how you, as a unique being, fit in with your group, or whether it's time to choose new social groups that honor, cherish, and support who you are.

Katie McCann, *Layers*, 2020, Collage on Book Cover, Doug + Laurie Kanyer Art Collection

Emily Marbach, *Love—Never Mind the Rest*, 2020, Collage, Doug + Laurie Kanyer Art Collection

Gems Documenting Profound Connections

"Follow your bliss and the universe will open doors where there were only walls."

—Joseph Campbell

GEM 48 ▷ **Collage Documents a Miracle**

Have you ever experienced a miracle? A miracle being an unexplainable event having some connection to the Divine. Many people have and their lives have been significantly changed. Regardless of the transformation they experience, many people hesitate to share miracles with others worrying they would not be believed. Sadly, instead of sharing a life changing miracle, many kept the miracle to themselves. The emotional tension of holding onto a miracle story can be burdensome. The weight of questioning one's self related to a fantastic, unexplainable event, can take its toll.

Collage can transform this experience by offering you a way to document the miracle in code using symbols only you can understand. You deserve to record, document, and process your miracles to appreciate the positive impact on your life. Many people I worked with trusted me and told me of miracles in their lives. We would make collages to document and magnify the truth of the miracles. They went from feeling uncertain about the experiences, to being amazed and believed in themselves even more. By making a collage about their miracles, each person felt the gift and blessing more fully.

Curiously, those I worked with began to look for more miracles to follow! Many eventually shared their collages documenting the miracles with those they trusted. They found in doing so, others shared they too had similar miraculous experiences, yet had hesitated to talk about the miracles with others. By making a collage and sharing it with others, the positive impact of the miracles can be amplified. Seeing is believing, and you can make a collage about the miracle in your life right now.

GEM 49 ▷ **Collage Offers Profound Bliss**

There can be a true Nirvana-like state that happens when you make a collage. You can become so lost in the creative process that you feel as though you're in another world. When you lose yourself in the process of making a collage, you shift into a state of momentary altered awareness that is often described as blissful. You are in your happy place. This can be said about anything one becomes passionate about, but with collage and its use of found items (magazines, books, objects) you can step into and enter another dimension by way of the materials. Like a cabinet of curiosities, when you make collages, your eyes invite you into another realm that you can get lost in. It's as though time is suspended and your current situation is forgotten—absorbed in the moment.

During my career as a counselor, I worked with many who were faced with a multitude of traumas and hardships. In my clinical observations, I saw how they would enter into the group feeling discouraged. However, after making collages during two-hour working sessions, they would leave the group in a much improved and elevated state. They seemed to float out of the room.

Making a collage allows you to experience euphoria, even if just for an hour or two, giving you the opportunity to hear the voice of your heart. Everything you're doing in that very moment becomes crystalized, magnified, and all-consuming, allowing the heaviness of your day-to-day life to disappear into the periphery. You experience a joy so deep you can hear the synapses in your brain click as neurons of joy connect and expand. When you make collage and it brings forth this depth of joy, you climb the ladder of self-actualization.

Keep an eye out, as those who are experiencing bliss often have increased experiences of synchronicity. Once you experience the bliss in making collage, a door of higher living and profound joy has been opened. You need only step through and be whisked away to another world on a cloud of blissful euphoria.

Niko Vartiainen, *My Saint*, 2013, Collage, Doug + Laurie Kanyer Art Collection

GEM 50 ▷ **Collage Uses Your Preferred Color to Get Your Point Across**

It might not occur to those working in collage, but you can use color to express your emotions. This is true, you can! Paper is your paint in collage, and you can use it in a way that will drive home the point of the collage with color rather than a literal object. It will indicate how you feel or what you recall about a life event in a different and impactful way. Let's say you're making a collage that involves a tree in the composition. Rather than eliciting an image of an actual tree, you can search for the colors of a tree instead, building it with various colored elements.

The focus of your search then shifts from looking for literal objects to looking for color, allowing you to practice a more abstract and creative thought process. It is in this kind of abstract thinking and seeing that you can really begin to broaden the creative possibilities for a deeper and more powerful expression of self. Color not only indicates physical appearances, it can also be used to convey emotion and mood.

I believe it is important to honor and respect your own intentions and meaning for your collage and avoid others' interpretations. Let's say you decide to make your tree entirely out of black elements. Based on your decision to use black, some might claim this indicates that you are in a dark mood. You should understand that whatever color you choose, you are the only one who knows and understands what it represents for you.

The interpretation of colors varies from one culture to the next, and the associations and meaning we attach to them can be more personal than universal. So choose whatever color you believe best conveys how you feel or what you think about a life event, person, place, or thing. You will find the application of color to be an indispensable tool for self-expression and discovery.

GEM 51 ▷ **Collage Explores Relationships with Materials and Connections to Things**

You can have relationships with things, places, and people. The concept related to a relationship with a place or environment is called place attachment (Shumaker & Taylor, 1983). For example, you can have a strong and deep relationship to a piece of jewelry, a car, or the home you grew up in. The relationship is in the meaning you attach to the object, which symbolizes an emotional connection for you.

Another example is when you make a collage and choose to use an image of a family member or a piece of cloth from a favorite shirt that is now threadbare. In this situation, you are using something that you have a relational connection. Oftentimes, the objects we hold near and dear are described as having sentimental value.

Your relationships with materials can be forged through personal preference, as well. Maybe you like to use a certain type of magazine, or maybe you prefer using digital images. Your preferences express your relationship with, and to, the material. This is important because you are describing yourself, your preferences, and endearments through your relationship with the materials you use. They become part of your artistic visual vocabulary, helping to convey your unique ways of working and being in the world. This vocabulary is both your expression of connection and your unique fingerprint. As you make collage, you begin to discover and develop your preferences, which bring forth a positive feeling tone and intention. This feeling tone can be described as love, and will likely bring forth an endorphin high. As you make collage with your preferred material, you ensure a positive feeling tone and sense of connection. This helps to create healthy neural pathways and well-being.

Lane, *What if, I agree with everyone?*, 2018, Collage, Doug + Laurie Kanyer Art Collection

Miss Printed, *2 + 2 = 5*, 2017, Collage, Doug + Laurie Kanyer Art Collection

Gems Enhancing Problem-Solving & Decision-Making

"We cannot solve our problems with
the same level of thinking
that created them."

—Albert Einstein

GEM 52 ▷ **Collage Supports Asking For Help**

Asking for help with problems is one sign of personal growth. It is a sophisticated social skill that demonstrates emotional balance. It shows you are humble and willing to show you don't know everything. It is an act of vulnerability that leads to collaborations with others, benefiting both you and them. It also makes you more approachable, as people see you as human.

When you were in your early childhood years, you may have asked for help often in order to survive. If and when your caregivers responded to those requests for help, they may have built trust with you, which taught you about love. Over time, you grew, and perhaps learned to do things independently. This independence may have built confidence in your own self-efficacy, increasing a sense of pride in using your skills. Being able to take care of oneself is an important phase in human development.

Additionally, you, like many others, may have been taught to believe you had to do it all by yourself once you developed that early sense of independence. Or maybe you did not receive help from others when you asked for it, which required you to rely only on yourself, as others had not worked to develop a sense of trust. As a result of being unexpectedly thrust into independence, you may have become somewhat stuck in adolescence, the human development phase commonly associated with the formation of individual identity.

Adulthood, though, is about interdependence and teamwork in all your relationships, whether they be romantic, friendly, vocational, or community-based. Asking for and offering help is vital to both the community and the individual. Being an adult means you can balance accomplishing things on your own with proficiency (independence) and needing help from others (interdependence).

Collage can help you develop a sense of interdependence as you practice asking for help. One way to do so is to make a collage about the thing you need support in doing. Place elements that represent the things you need, take a step back, and identify as many people who can help as a way to create a bank of supporters. Find the following words in your source materials and cut them out as an element to place on the collage: "I need some help from you. Can you help me or shall I ask someone else?" Know you are strong, and asking for help shows your strength.

GEM 53 ▷ **Collage Affirms You Can Solve Problems**

When you're searching for elements to use in your collage and you discover just the right piece, it affirms and proves your ability to solve problems and reminds you of times in the past when you have successfully solved problems before. As you start collaging, you are facing a puzzle, a problem needing to be solved. Your task is to start to find the elements and make a pleasing arrangement. Your confidence will explode and become clear as you successfully locate elements to show what you plan to illustrate while making an arrangement you love.

When you are making a collage, you are involved in the act of problem-solving. As you address the task of making the collage and find elements, you prove that, without a doubt, you can address and solve problems. This confronts and dissolves prior beliefs you may have about your abilities, while quieting the feeling of helplessness you may experience when faced with an overwhelming problem. Then, if you are faced with struggles in other areas of your life, you might choose to carry your collage with you as a tangible reminder that you can problem-solve.

Laurence Briat, *Fragile*, 2020, Collage, Doug + Laurie Kanyer Art Collection

GEM 54 ▷ Collage Reveals the Exact Problem Needing to be Addressed

Making a collage offers you the chance to non-verbally clarify the problem or life experience you are facing. There are times when a picture can illustrate a problem more clearly than words can. For example, medical practitioners might use a FACES rating (Wong & Baker, 1983) to give patients a facial representation of their pain intensity. The patient can simply point to the face that shows their pain level. This helps the care team to assess and tend to their patient in an appropriate and speedy manner.

When you choose elements representing all of the aspects contributing to the emotional upheaval, the resulting collage can show exactly what you are dealing with and bring the issue in clear view. No words are needed. Others will be able to decipher the meaning of the images on the collage and assist in helping you. This process transforms the conversations you are having with yourself, too. It allows you to be specific and focus on the true concern, rather than spinning in uncertainty. You and others can get an eagle's eye view on the concern. This will give you an opportunity to handle the problem based on what you discover instead of guessing.

GEM 55 ▷ Collage Inspires New Ideas and Offers Miraculous, Endless Possibilities

In order to solve problems, you will need to find a variety of resources, help, and information. You have to go on a scavenger hunt. As you look through the source material to find elements for your collage, you will come across some novel ideas—new information and possible solutions to help you with problems you are facing. Your source material will be filled with articles or stories of others who have solved problems. It will tell you exactly what they did to alleviate a concern.

It is truly a mystery—when one engages in problem-solving, admits they need help, and begins actively searching for ideas—the solutions seem to magically appear. You see, the act of searching, while certainly painful and frustrating, sets forth an energy field of possibilities. Time and time again people have jaw-dropping experiences when making collage—they search, turn a page, and BAM! By miracle, or magic, or synchronicity, right there in front of them is an answer.

There are forces out there advocating for good in your life, and you can be the co-creator in the journey. Committing to creative endeavors like collage serves to unlock endless possibilities and answers. When you make a collage, you are linking parts of your brain to spark the transfer of creative energy to discover solutions you have not yet considered. Please just turn the page, make the collage, and keep looking. New ideas are just around the cover of the next magazine.

GEM 56 ▷ Collage Shows the Complexity of an Octopus Problem

Making a collage offers you the chance to examine the complexity of a problem. Some problems are like an octopus with many tangled tentacles of conflicting input going different directions in your mind. Octopus problems can be so complex one needs to use an image to comprehend, analyze, and decipher all the details related to the problem.

You can manage a problem that is incredibly complex by selecting a single element for each part of the problem. Each element can represent each aspect of the problem, giving you some space to examine it all. The resulting collage can reveal insights into the magnitude of the issue. This gives you insight as to why you feel so confused or overwhelmed by what is taking place. Seeing is believing! This process will grow your sense of self-compassion as you navigate all you are going through and see all the elements connected to the problem in the same place.

Danielle Cole, *Let's Clean This Place Up*, 2017, Collage, Doug + Laurie Kanyer Art Collection

You will come to accept how complicated the situation really is as you view your collage. You will literally be able to see the octopus-of-a-problem and begin to wrap your arms around it as you examine each aspect influencing the concern. This will give you an opportunity to address the issue—one element, or arm of the octopus, at a time—based on what you discover. You will be able to take one step at a time, in a paced and thoughtful manner to solve the concern. You might label the arms of the problem (what needs to be done) in numerical order and even set a possible time frame for implementation of solutions, too.

This process will reduce your stress and quiet feelings of confusion. You will go from dealing with a slippery, tangled octopus problem that seems burdensome to adding structure to the problem by dealing with one element at a time. You will be able to solve all the bits in smaller, more manageable pieces, quieting the tendency to multi-task and reduce the feelings of being overwhelmed.

GEM 57 ▷ **Collage Magnifies a Promise**

In many Hollywood movies people would make promises to each other saying, "My word is my bond." They would cement the promise with a handshake and off they would ride on horseback into the sunset. Seems unlikely they would follow through. To fully ground a promise one needs to make a visual contract and a collage can be the answer.

When you make a declaration that you will accomplish something or halt from doing something—to yourself or another—you need to do so on paper or collage, with words or symbols (elements) showing what you are going to do. This will transform the feeling of intention into action to do what you promise. Making a collage about your promise to yourself or another means you have taken the first step of a contract of sorts. In making a promise collage you move beyond just words and a handshake to engaging yourself in the creation of a vow coming alive. It becomes a visual reminder to help hold you accountable to address a promise or an issue. You can also track the progress of your promise on the opposite side of the collage, gluing elements down on a timeline to document your headway toward fulfilling the promise.

GEM 58 ▷ **Collage Expands Options—Motivates You to Keep Looking for Solutions**

When you make a collage, you take seemingly unrelated elements from different sources in order to create something complete and new.

This is much like the process of problem-solving. You research and get ideas from various people and resources, weigh your options, and decide which is the right one to solve your concern. When you get stuck while making a collage and you feel as though you just can't find the right elements, you are motivated to keep looking until you do. In making a collage, you are practicing your problem-solving skills while affirming that you can continue searching for answers and creative new solutions.

GEM 59 ▷ **Collage Can Tackle a Number of Problems at the Same Time**

It is common for you to face a number of important concerns or projects at once, all of which need to be addressed. Not only are you facing the feelings about each concern individually, but you might feel increased anxiety and confusion due to the sheer number of problems.

To help ease the strain and offer you a clearer focus, you can make separate collages for each issue you are experiencing. You can create a separate collage for each coinciding concern. This will help you to get a clearer visual on what each individual problem actually is, while affirming the strain you are going through.

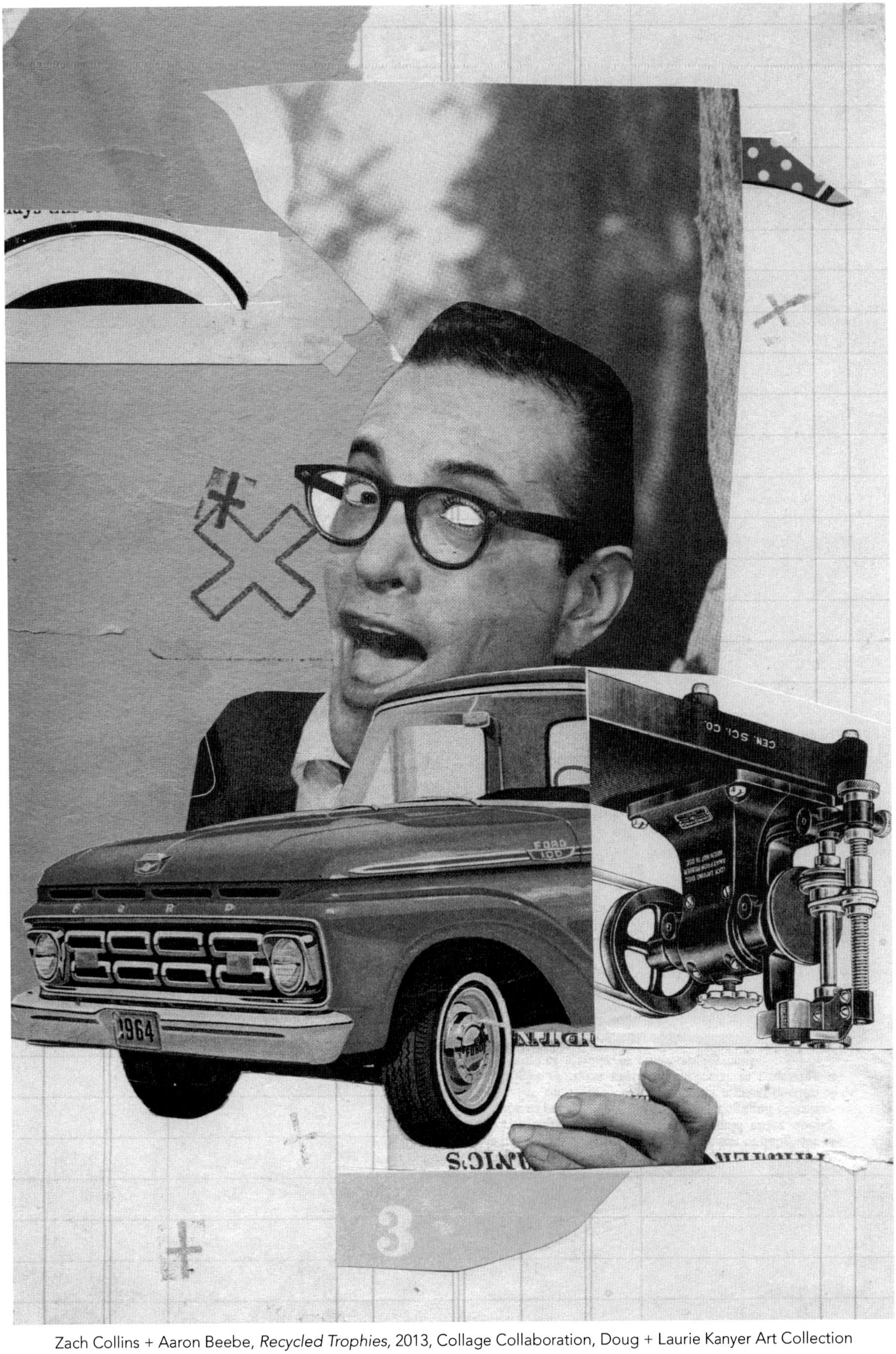

Zach Collins + Aaron Beebe, *Recycled Trophies,* 2013, Collage Collaboration, Doug + Laurie Kanyer Art Collection

You will begin to understand why you may be feeling so frazzled and engulfed in disorientation. Making separate collages for each concern allows you to see them collectively, side by side, giving you the opportunity to consider your problems with clarity, rather than letting them tumble around in your mind. This process will free up your cluttered headspace, reduce your stress levels by clearly identifying your concerns, allow you to address them, and communicate to others the magnitude of the pressure you are enduring.

GEM 60 ▷ **Collage Helps You to Make Decisions and Commit**

As you build your collage, you will be faced with a multitude of decisions, much like daily life. Eventually, you have to make a choice and commit. Collage helps to strengthen your ability to make decisions as you choose elements to address a concern or life experience and shows that you can commit to your decisions when you glue the elements down. This is a practice that can be extended to real-life problems.

In making a collage, you are witnessing yourself making choices and committing to your decisions. This will fortify your confidence to make decisions and commit to them beyond the page of your collage.

GEM 61 ▷ **Collage Supports the Three Day Rule**

Have you ever been in a situation and you felt you needed to solve the problem immediately? The pressure is on! Some people have a low tolerance for the discomfort a situation can bring. They have to do something and get it off their plate, as it can be so hard to regulate the emotions connected to the problem. Or people in your circle may be urging you to do something. You may feel the pressure to please them in order to get them off your back! But, hear this—it takes time to identify solutions that will actually work and last long-term.

There is an alternative to going into overdrive in the attempt to please people—simply wait for three days, make a collage, and see if the problem just works itself out. There is no magic to this method. Putting the situation to the side for a while has worked for many, especially when making collage. The idea of waiting to see, observe, take notes, and give the universe time to offer a solution is a remarkable habit.

Having waited for three days, you can't be faulted with moving too soon—for overreacting. You will also have the added benefit of three nights' sleep to organize your thoughts as you dream. And having let the potency of the initial emotions melt away when you made the collage, you will be more prepared to proceed. The practice of making a collage, while you pause to let a solution present itself, will help you to flex your patience muscles and avoid the overreaction that can come in the heat of the moment. Give it three days!

> *Note: This applies to non-emergency situations. If you are in crisis or danger, this three day rule does not apply–please seek immediate support by calling 911, 800-273-8255, or texting HOME to 741741 (United States), 85258 (United Kingdom), or 50808 (Ireland)!*

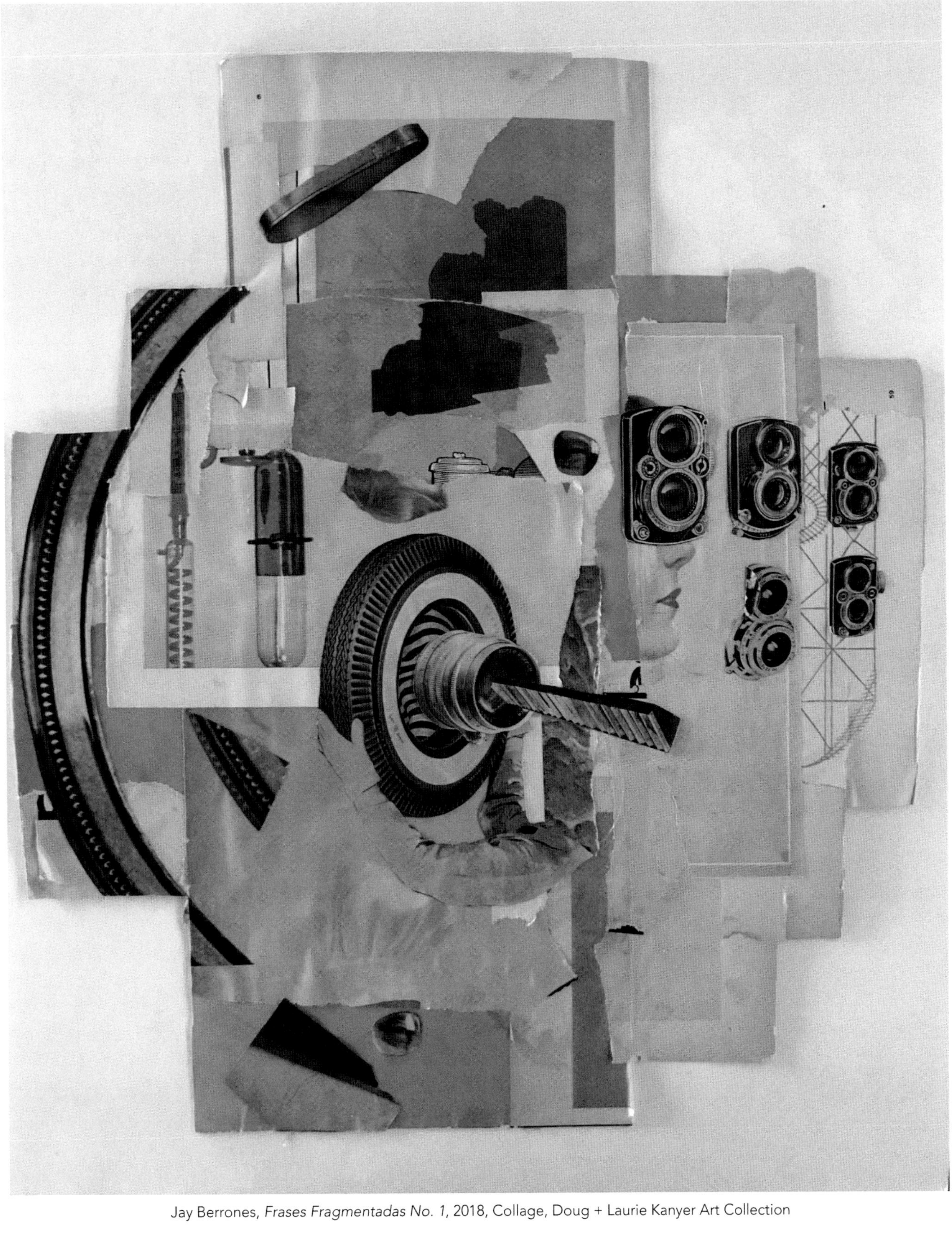

Jay Berrones, *Frases Fragmentadas No. 1*, 2018, Collage, Doug + Laurie Kanyer Art Collection

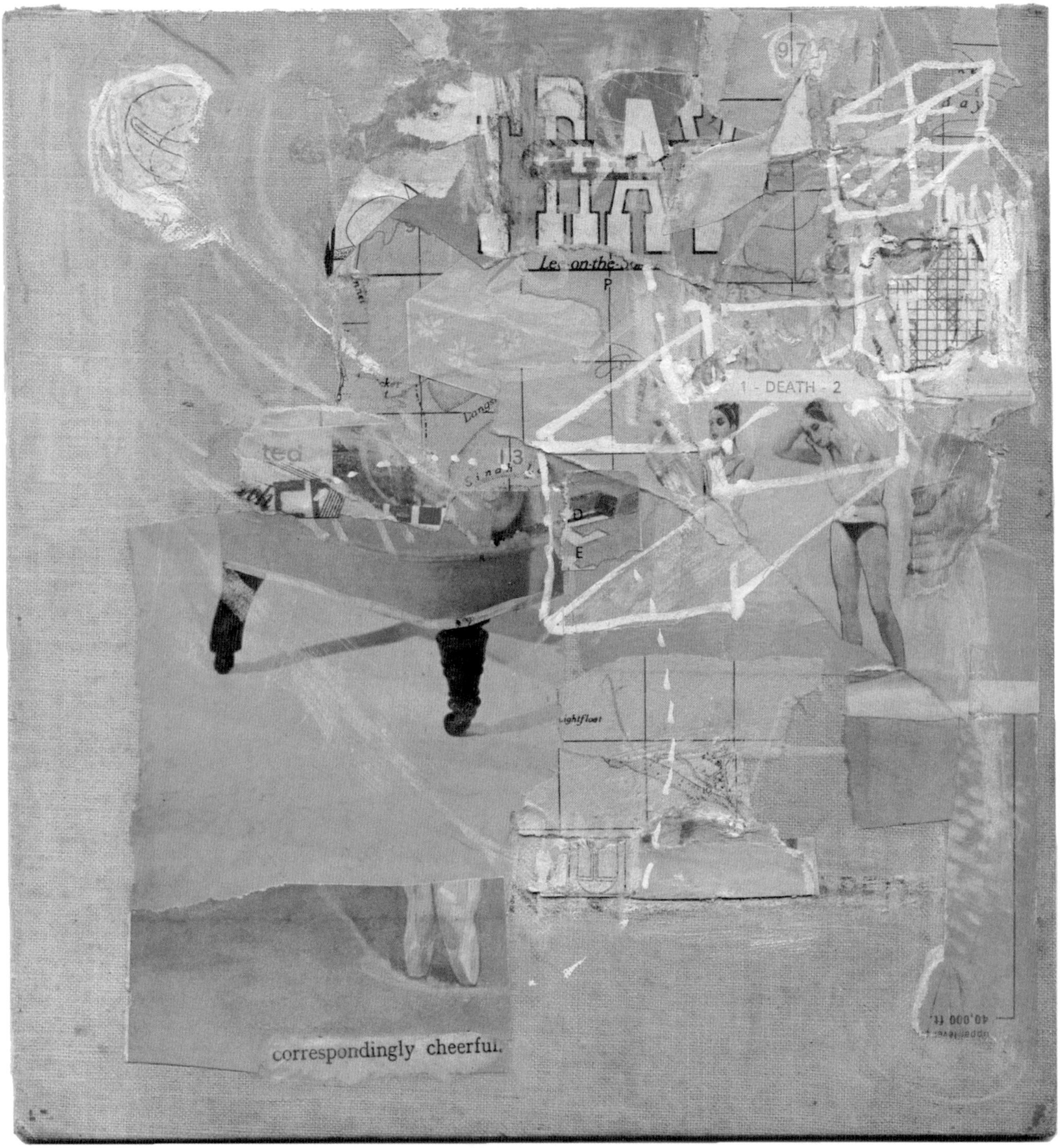

Oliver Lunn, *Correspondingly Cheerful Death*, 2019, Collage on Inside of Book Cover, Doug + Laurie Kanyer Art Collection

Gems Documenting Your Life

"Our childhood memories are often fragments, brief moments or encounters, which together form the scrapbook of our life."

—Edith Eger

GEM 62 ▷ **Collage Shows Renewal**

You will go through periods or cycles of renewal over the course of your life—a recycled pattern of beginnings, growth, rest, renewal, and transformation. Collage starts with material that, in so many ways, is on this same path. For instance, the magazine itself is experiencing a new beginning as it's being used for your collage. As the collage develops and grows, it mirrors what it was like for you as you developed and grew during a transformative moment. Considering this can soothe your life transitions and help you to recognize your ongoing growth.When you take a period of time away from your collage, it echoes the times of rest, gestation, and renewal you have experienced before in life, as well as the plateaus in your development.

Do you remember being 14 years old and everything seemed so confusing? Just like that strange and often difficult transitional period in your life, as you build a collage, you will experience moments of transformation that may feel awkward and confusing. As you make more collages, this process of development repeats like times of your own development, even into adulthood. Collage shows you the growing pains and the finished phases of human development—your very life. It will help you to feel a sense of comfort and renewal at times when things seem off for some unknown reason.

GEM 63 ▷ **Collage Builds a Legacy**

The collages you make, which have emotional significance for you, may very well come to pull on others' heartstrings—those being people who will come after you. Right now, it may be difficult to imagine, but others will be interested in your life after you've passed. These people will come to treasure your collages and have a broader picture of your life. Your collages will become part of what you leave behind, your legacy to be mined, explored, and appreciated by those who remain. These people may choose to follow in your footsteps. They may even use your collages as material to build their own collages, carrying on the long tradition of repurposing found images to create a collage.

Another interesting thing to note is that collage is swiftly gaining honor and respect in the art world. Art historians like Dr. Freya Gowrley and Dr. Cole Collins are the conveyors of the Collage Research Network, dedicated solely to the study and advancement of understanding the history of collage. These scholars have devoted their careers to the study of this incredible medium, holding symposiums, writing scholarly papers, and more. In making contemporary collages created on the topics of emotions and relationships now, you are making historical art for the future. As mentioned before, according to Anila Babla, who wrote an article featured on the Collage Research Network website, we are in the fourth developmental phase of collage as an art form, that being the exploration of one's self (Babla, A., 2020). As you make your collages to explore your life experiences, you are making your own personal contribution to both art history and your own future legacy.

GEM 64 ▷ **Collage Shows History and can be a Private Diary**

Just as the layers of your collage can represent historical layers of your life, collectively your collages can tell your life story. Many collagists use a sketchbook in their art practice to work on their skills or sort out a technical problem. You can use a sketchbook and it can act as a diary—a visual record of your life. This is deeply beneficial to mark your existence and offer you a safe space where you can be completely honest and tell your story. A collage diary is also confidential, as others will not know the real meaning of the collage.

Teri Fridley, *Communication*, 2020, Doug + Laurie Kanyer Art Collection

A collage diary is an excellent way to extend your relationship with yourself while having a window into your day-to-day life. Your collage diary can also be more like a scrapbook where you keep sentimental things, such as tickets from events or cards you receive from others. You can record ideas or life events, adding things later to further evaluate your experiences.

Some collagists may use a new blank sketchbook, but others might use an old book they love and collage right on top of the words. This is an interesting way to blend your story with the stories of others, and it mirrors real life. You could even choose to use your favorite childhood book or a novel you love to collage. No matter how you choose to do it, the emotional value of keeping a collage diary is incredibly deep because you are putting your life in storybook form, which can be shared and examined for generations to come.

GEM 65 ▷ **Collage Marks Important Milestones**

When you reflect back on your life or as you move into the future, there will be key milestones and important events to honor and mark. It is beneficial to have a way to make note of all the important times in your life so you can recall them in the years to come. In making collages regarding these milestone moments, you are creating a record that will help you to track your growth, appreciate your life phases, and consider the things you've learned, showing you existed, and illustrating your transformations.

A collection of collages about your life can become a visual biography that will help to address some of the feelings and notions you have about yourself, the weighty and joyous events you experienced.

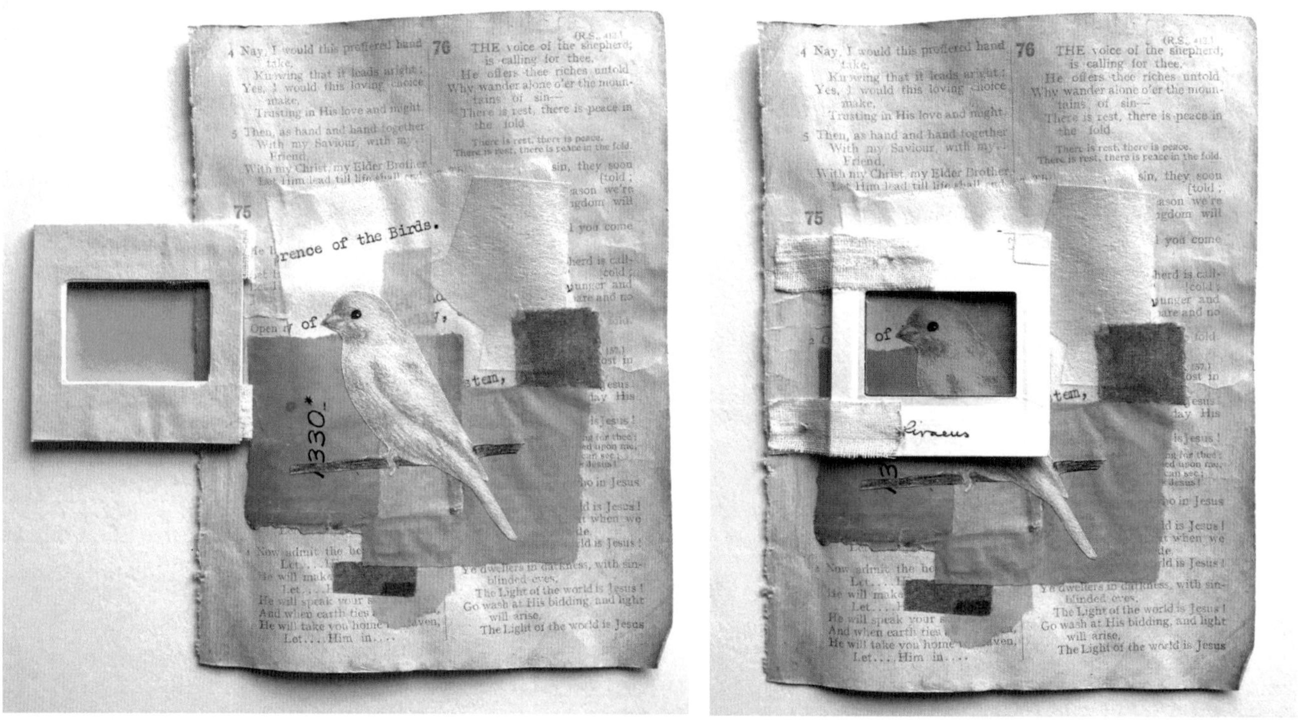

Jane Chipp, *Canary*, 2020, Collage, Doug + Laurie Kanyer Art Collection

Rocio Romero, *Paper Lover*, 2020, Collage, Doug + Laurie Kanyer Art Collection

Meikel Church, *Another Chance*, 2016, Collage, Doug + Laurie Kanyer Art Collection

Gems Affirming Self-Efficacy & Personal Strengths

"In order to succeed, people need a sense of self-efficacy, to struggle together with resilience to meet the inevitable obstacles and inequities of life."

—Albert Bandura

GEM 66 ▷ **Collage Decreases Helplessness—Inspires Hope**

When faced with circumstances where you feel helpless, you can show yourself you can move mountains by putting one in a collage. Go ahead and put a person on top of that mountain to represent yourself standing proudly after having travailed the challenging climb!

The feeling of helplessness is connected to situations where one feels that nothing can improve how things are or that they can't control a situation. When you make a collage, you move from feeling helpless to hopeful. Hope consists of engaging your will, making a commitment, and tapping into your motivation to accomplish a task. Hope is an active process, and making a collage is the perfect way to ignite and illustrate hope while demonstrating your self-efficacy.

You can make a hope collage to address the feeling of helplessness. Hope is something profoundly beautiful and powerful in the mind. Put elements on the collage to show your will, your commitment, and motivation! Climb that mountain, and take the first step today.

GEM 67 ▷ **Collage Demonstrates Self-Efficacy and Mastery**

Self-efficacy is the personal belief in your ability to have influence over your life, to make progress in those things that are key and important to you. Making a collage offers you the chance to show your self-efficacy and proves you can put things in the order you intend. As you make collages and gain proficiency in your collage skills, it illustrates your ability to master challenges and make accomplishments in your life. It has a powerful influence in how you feel, think, make decisions, and carry out tasks.

Collage offers you a way to have control, as you get to choose the people, places, or things in your collage that you find pleasing and inspiring. This shows your ability to follow through on your intentions and illustrates your power to do so. With each collage you make, you will enhance your belief in yourself and your inner strength—you can see it right there on the collage.

GEM 68 ▷ **Collage Highlights the Value of Gluing**

Have you ever hammered a nail into two pieces of wood, connecting them just as you intended? Then you know the satisfying feeling of making connections, or putting things together just as you planned and desired. With every strike of the hammer, you have evidence of your ability to influence something. This is how it is with collage, too. You are the being, the very soul, making the connections by gluing the elements together. It is like you have the power to place the stars in the night sky. You are the one doing it! You are the one who is gluing the elements together, assigning meaning to the collage.

The origin of the word *collage* is from Old French coller, meaning to glue, and making a collage offers you a chance to symbolically cement things together, even when life seems to be falling apart. This will help you feel more grounded, or glued together, yourself. Collage is the perfect tool to help you manage abundant changes and daily ongoing strains.

The act of gluing, like hammering the nail, demonstrates your potent self-efficacy, as you are able to build, create, make shifts, and impact your world. It will help to dissolve your feelings of helplessness and replace them with a newfound sense of control.

Celia Crane, *It's Hard to See the Picture When You're Inside the Frame*, 2020, Collage, Doug + Laurie Kanyer Art Collection

GEM 69 ▷ **Collage Allows You to be Your Own Superhero—Improves Self-Esteem**

When you feel small and insignificant, collage can help you to create a visual image of your inner superhero, illustrating ways for you to imagine yourself handling difficult and frustrating, maybe even scary situations. This will improve your mental awareness of your capacity to be strong, capable, caring, and goal-focused.

Some of the character traits of superheroes are as follows: they are clear about their mission, they are focused on their goal, they work until the task is completed, they right wrongs, and they help others. Superheroes experience hardship and are inspired to move beyond these life challenges. They practice deep belief in themselves and are willing to take on responsibility. They are disciplined in practicing their superhero skills and work hard. They attempt to do their very best, even when the odds are against them. They stop and think in order to have the strength to endure. They are humble, not seeking attention, and yet they know their personal power. They are fully human and do make mistakes from time to time. While they are capable of independent accomplishment, they know the benefit of working with others and asking for help.

Superheroes have a strong sense of right and wrong and set lofty goals to accomplish unimaginable feats. They are aware of the parts of themselves and the role that they play in the world, too. SUPERHERO! In making a collage of a superhero and having it in your world, you will be able to have a reminder of your own super powers, adopting the character traits of superheroes and their capabilities.

GEM 70 ▷ **Collage Offers a Chance to Evaluate—Controls the Drama**

If your life is full of drama caused by others, making a collage offers you a chance to be the author or director of the situation instead of waiting for others to do it. It also gives you a chance to step off the Drama Triangle and avoid triangulation. You may have people in your life who intentionally set out to stir the pot of your existence. They find something to create dramatic episodes on a regular basis. While you can't change others' actions, you can make a collage featuring the way you would like the situation to turn out or to show your efforts to avoid drama. In making a collage, you can design an ending to the situation that would fit best for you, helping you to feel grounded and practicing options to offer others when more drama evolves.

You can make a collage tracing the most recent series of dramatic events with someone to affirm and confirm what you are experiencing—to know you are not imagining what is taking place. By making a collage about the drama, you will be able to determine patterns you observe and detect how the events of this relationship may trigger you, causing you to have an intense response.

You can make a collage about practicing how to ask people to shift their patterns of behavior, asking for change. In doing so, you will discover ideas about how to handle your response moving forward in order to actualize your desired outcomes, decreasing the potency of the situation. Additionally, you may gain compassion for the other person, as the creative process will give you the ability to consider their perspective, allowing for insights into what is driving their behavior. Make a collage as a shield to guard against drama today.

Peter Dowker, *ON POINT*, 2016, Collage, Doug + Laurie Kanyer Art Collection

GEM 71 ▷ **Collage Creates Opportunities for Taking Charge—Reconfigures Your Life**

Have you ever just wanted to start over—fire your life, move to another city, another country, another planet—and begin anew? It might feel like you are burning up all your energy, spinning in circles, and not getting where you want to go. You may feel stuck with a group of people or a dissatisfying job that feels like a waste of precious life. You may realize that your emotional status is compromised by the repetitious and futile efforts to improve your life.

Collage can help you, as it offers a way to document your current reality and then disassemble the parts of that reality that bring pain and suffering. If you are frustrated and feeling stuck in your current world configuration, you can make a collage about your life and literally cut or tear the collage up and reassemble it the way you want.

The act of deconstruction will allow for a cathartic expulsion of related feelings that stick with you when experiencing a rut. Making a collage about your experience will be a new thing to do, instead of the same old thing repeatedly, expecting different results. It will fortify your sense of power in what seems like an otherwise powerless situation. You will visually see this new arrangement, which will demonstrate that you can create new possibilities, discover different life paths, and explore exciting opportunities.

GEM 72 ▷ **Collage Gives You Something-to-Do When You Feel Like Nothing Can-be-Done**

Sometimes you may feel as if there is nothing that can be done to improve a situation. You may be going through a period of forced waiting that feels like it has gone on forever, which can be especially excruciating and ignite anxiety. Times like this can interfere with your productivity as your mind floats to the situation distracting you.

Collage will give you something to do while you wait, planting seeds of hope and commitment, dissolving feelings of helplessness. It will help you fill the space of time between the start of the situation and the final outcome. Doing something that feels productive while you wait will quiet feelings of wasting time and allow you to have some fun. In addition, you may come up with some ideas to assist the strain at hand and you will likely make something beautiful.

You will witness completing something and it will renew your sense of self-efficacy. Your collage will become a symbolic reminder of your ability to be patient, which is an important character trait. If you are waiting with others, it can be especially wonderful to invite them to make a collage with you, too.

GEM 73 ▷ **Collage Helps You Learn and Practice Skills**

There are an abundance of simple collage techniques and affordable books that demonstrate easy ways to make remarkable collages. You can take an online class to gain more insight. Most methods are simple approaches, but create impressive visual impact.

Over time, you will witness yourself growing in your proficiency using your scissors, finding pleasing compositions, and illustrating your ideas on the substrate. When you explore new collage methods, acquiring and practicing new skill sets, you can build confidence and feel more capable in other areas of your life, too. And because collage is nearly free, you won't have to stress about spending a great deal of money to experience the benefits. As you gain deeper insight and skill in collage, you will naturally become curious about other things in life. Collage can ignite passions and desires to learn other skills. If you feel inspired to learn more, you can refer to the suggested Resources in the back of this book.

Monique Vettraino, *Otherworldly*, 2019, Collage, Doug + Laurie Kanyer Art Collection

GEM 74 ▷ **Collage Shows the Value of Small Steps**

When you add elements to your collage, you witness how each small step and gesture adds up and has a collective impact on the finished collage. You have evidence that even the smallest of steps cumulatively contributes to the bigger picture, just as increasing your water intake and adding a walk to your daily-care regimen will support your overall health. This is a dynamic message that can remind you that you are making an enormous impact, no matter how small or incremental a step might be.

Like doing a puzzle, consisting of a multitude of pieces, collage will compel you to find the will to take steps, even if they seem to be tiny and challenging. Sometimes a 1,000-piece jigsaw puzzle suddenly takes form after someone connects one piece—maybe it's a tree branch, a swatch of sunset, or a person's shoe. This transformation might take place after identifying the puzzle's border or boundaries, too. While this single piece (or boundary formation process) represents one of one-thousand steps toward completing the task at hand, it can also be the catalyst for transformation.

Seeing how each element contributes to the larger project can be transferred to other areas of your life, strengthening your sense of self-efficacy. With each element placed, you have a record of your effort to create and contribute. Every step counts!

Jim Ford, *Inkblot 25*, Collage, Doug + Laurie Kanyer Art Collection

Juliette Pestel, *Whatever Works*, 2020, Collage on Book Cover, Doug + Laurie Kanyer Art Collection

Roberta Guarna, *Finding a Place of My Own*, 2019, Collage, Doug + Laurie Kanyer Art Collection

Gems Exploring Memories

"The faculty of memory cannot be separated from the imagination. They go hand in hand. To one degree or another, we all invent our personal pasts. And for most of us those pasts are built from emotionally colored memories."

—Siri Hustsvedt

GEM 75 ▷ **Collage Explores Memories and Identity**

Like the processing and transformation of feelings, collage offers a quick and efficient way to reflect on life experiences and the memories attached to them. Think of a memory as information filed and stored in the brain. We know there is a system in the care and tending of memories, which consists of encoding, storing, and recalling information (National Institute for the Clinical Application of Behavioral Medicine, 2017). Like any system of storage, there is both the process (implicit memory, which consists of emotional and procedural memory) and content (explicit memory, which consists of semantic and episodic memory) (NICABM, 2017). Additionally, you might notice that your memories have a fluid quality when you access them. You might find recent and past memories connecting, like a small stream connecting to a river. This can be a random process where unrelated memories flow together, or reconsolidate (Miller, 2010). Those moments where the memory streams commingle and merge together could form a fresh memory—a tributary of sorts—in real time. This association of two possibly unrelated experiences may have formed a new memory with new elements (Miller, 2010).

There is a sensory component to memories, too. You experience this when you hear a song and it takes you back to your high school days, or when you catch a fragrance in the air and you're suddenly in your grandmother's kitchen (Menakem, 2017). Often people think memories are only about sentimental things—loving or harsh—but memories are so much more than that. You can hear, smell, taste, or see something that activates a memory of a difficult or joyful time, too.

From an emotional and mental health perspective, the consideration of memories is important as they shape your self-identity. Identity is how you see and understand yourself to be. It is your sense of self, providing you with sameness and continuity in personality over time. Identity is a script or operating system for your worth and abilities. With collage, you are given visual and sensory cues that tap into this operating system. You can see, feel, smell, and hear the fragments of paper as you build a collage, offering you a profound way to access what you remember about an event or situation.

Rather than operate from outmoded perceptions you identified with in the past, you can explore your memories with a newfound maturity, reconsidering the validity of the conclusions, beliefs, and decisions you've made and the experiences you've navigated and survived. Collage will offer you a chance to confirm a memory to be accurate and help you recall details or aspects that would otherwise be forgotten. Using collage to explore your memories, you will gain a deeper understanding of your experiences. You will also gain understanding about the decisions and conclusions you make regarding yourself, other people, and the world you are immersed in.

GEM 76 ▷ **Collage Allows for Mindful Reflection of Memories**

Collage allows for the gift of time in the present to unveil new insights and ideas about issues, events, and life experiences you are having. When collage is used to engage with an issue, you contemplate and consider the aspects for an undetermined period of time by arranging and rearranging your chosen related elements. This will offer you a chance to practice what is called mindfulness, when you are in the here and now, considering your situation from a bird's eye view without attachment to outcome or assessment. You can also postpone permanently gluing your elements down until you have settled the situation, or you can have a collection of key elements, which are never permanent, to use for this purpose.

Clare Celeste Börsch, *Study In White*, 2018, Collage, Doug + Laurie Kanyer Art Collection

GEM 77 ▷ **Collage Offers Insight to Decades Past**

As you search for elements to make your collages, you will generally be using older materials published some time ago. This will naturally invite you to reflect upon and consider your past experiences. You will see older articles and advertisements from decades prior and gain knowledge of what was taking place in the world years ago. You will be able to know more about some of the prevalent attitudes shaping how people thought and behaved.

You will be exposed to the styles of a specific era and gain insights on—for example—the opinions previous generations held about clothing styles. In the 1940s, men of all income levels wore hats. In the mid-1920s flapper garb—made to be loose-fitting without a cinched waist—became a way for women to liberate from the restrictive corsets of the decades before.

As you scan vintage magazines, you have an opportunity to evaluate and compare life patterns of today with that of the past. This will allow you to gain understanding of what shaped ideas from years past and to see the origins of some concepts which are still held onto to this day.

Collage-making will give you a chance to ponder what you and others have experienced during your respective eras. It may prompt you to consider changes in your previous ways of thinking or fortify changes that you're working on. This will also foster appreciation for how far you have come in life and motivation to keep going!

GEM 78 ▷ **Collage Records a Dream**

When you have a dream that you can't quite remember or would like to decipher, you can make a collage about all the various elements; such as the people you were with, the places where you went, and even things that were said. As poet John O' Donohue wrote, "A dream is a drama we send to ourselves" (Tippet, n.d.). Whether the collage is sequential or random, the images help you to process the dream. It can aid you in recalling more details and assign meaning and value, if you choose.

There are abundant theories on the purpose and process of dreaming. There is still so much to learn, but what we do know for sure is that dreams can be heavy, confusing, and truly frightening. On the other hand, they can be joyful, funny, and delightful. Some can even seem to have a story or narrative to them, while others are puzzling and make absolutely no sense.

One idea on the purpose of dreams is that they help to organize or defragment aspects of your daily life, offering your brain a chance to tidy things up, so to speak. It is much like straightening up your physical or digital desktop after a big project. Dreaming helps you filter through all the events of the day and in some cases, your life. This creates an organized system of memories, experiences, and emotions in the brain. Another thought is that dreams help to address some aspects of your thinking process that you are avoiding or repressing. Regardless of all the notions, we know that some dreams stick with us upon waking, causing a stress in our day.

In making a collage, you can potentially decrease the potency of an unsettling dream and temper its haunting grip. It will help you to mine the story of what you have dreamed and see if there are themes to be further considered. You can simply record your dreams, as a way of deepening your relationship with yourself. If nothing more, this recording can be an excellent practice for self-exploration, discovery, and knowledge.

Kerith Lisi, *Inside 4 Calm*, 2020, Collage, Doug + Laurie Kanyer Art Collection

GEM 79 ▷ **Collage Finds Your Personal Truths**

When you hear a group of people recount a shared event or experience, you will also hear varying recollections from each, if not completely different stories altogether. Although everyone in the group experiences the same event, each person has their own perception, uniquely shaped by their temperament, sensory, and cognitive experiences. This experience might be considered equifinality, or the idea that a shared conclusion can be reached by a variety of methods and approaches (Bertalanffy, 1968). These experiences are what memories are made of.

Everyone has their own storage system for their memories. Your memories, in effect, form your personal truths, what you know to be real in the world around you. Some bits of information are collective truths and are shared by all. We agree the sky is blue and that grass is green, but how a person interprets the sky and the grass and the meanings they assign are personal. This inherent and unavoidable misperception occurs all the time and plays a huge role in why people so often feel misunderstood. One person's truth is not necessarily another's. Collage offers you a chance to decrease this confusion. You can make a collage about a perplexing situation you recall that is causing you to feel confused, misunderstood, and stressed out. It will allow you first to document what you know, or think you know. You can then analyze what you remember and talk to others, cross-referencing their memory of things with yours. The ability to analyze situations from multiple perspectives will help to clear up misunderstandings to address the issues so you can move on.

Remember, you are continuously evolving and shifting. Others are shifting, too. You are not the same person you were when some of your memories were formed and stored. By making a collage, you can get a clearer picture of your memories, helping you to move forward, revise, change your mind, and rewrite your understanding of self and others. The collage allows you to take the contents of the memory out of its file and sort through it, discarding what isn't helpful, keeping what is accurate, revising here and there and adding new insight!

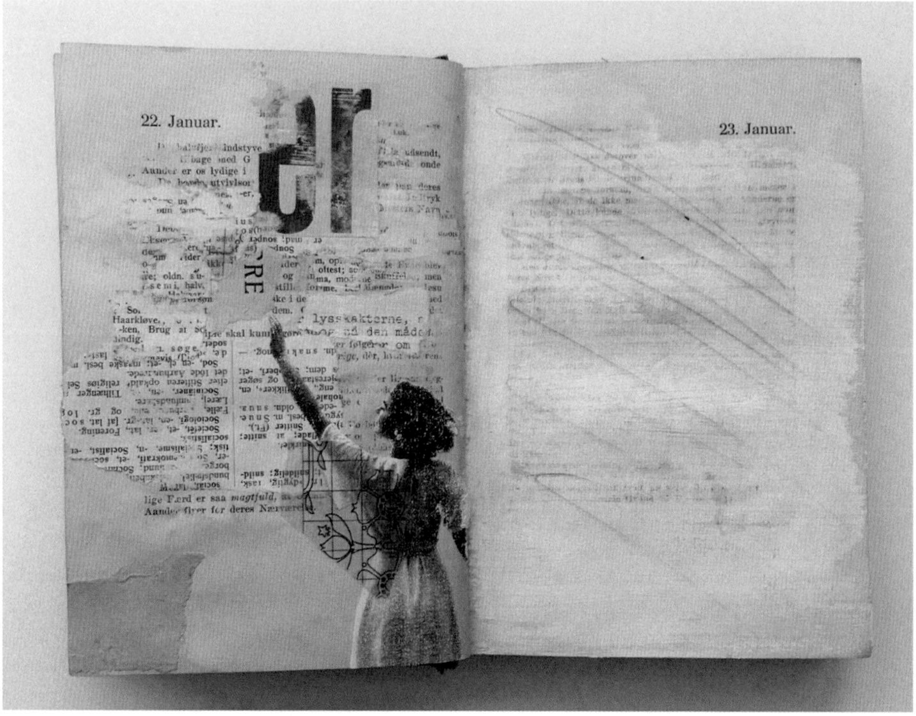

Anne Misfeldt, *Now*, 2021, Collage on Sketchbook Page, Courtesy of the Artist

Frances Ryan, *If You Promise to Arrive*, 2020, Collage, Doug + Laurie Art Collection

Antonio Guerra Alvarez, *Mujer entre pajaros regalo*, 2018, Digital Collage, Doug + Laurie Kanyer Art Collection

Gems Considering Relationships

"The meeting of two personalities is like the
contact of two chemical substances:
if there is any reaction, both
are transformed."

—Carl Gustav Jung

GEM 80 ▷ **Collage Illustrates Bonds**

The deep interpersonal connections you have with others, including animals, are forged through experiences of love and togetherness. We are created to have deep interpersonal bonds. Even during times of hardship and strain, emotional bonds of connection can be formed. Much like connecting the dots between the stars to create a constellation, as you glue the elements of your collage together, you will be inspired to consider the various connections and attachments that form the bond you have with others.

As you make the collage, you will be inspired to consider those you have relationships with, and those you would like to connect with, too. While using your creative imagination, you will become deeply grounded in contemplation about your relationships. This will fortify your connection with others and help build a stronger bond of togetherness. It will remind you to cherish and honor those in your life and identify ways to uplift and strengthen the glue that binds you.

As you use glue to attach elements to the collage, you will be able to reflect on the attachments you have and the deep bonds of affection to others. Collage can fortify and reawaken your ability to be intimate and form deep bonds with those you love. Your collage can become a love letter!

GEM 81 ▷ **Collage Evaluates Relationships**

You can make a collage to aid in the important task of evaluating the quality of a relationship. It can be refreshing and life-giving to take time to consider who you spend your life with—those precious minutes and hours that will never come again. You deserve to have experiences in relationships—especially those you have a choice in—that are uplifting and supportive. You can find others to spend your time with who are respectful, responsible, and pleasant to be around (Dawson, 1994), who encourage and care for you in nurturing ways.

In choosing elements to represent both the positive and negative aspects of a relationship, you create a clear visual that you can evaluate and weigh in on. You can explore events, actions, and conversations exchanged that may have been heavy, uncomfortable, or confusing. You can look objectively to see if this person is someone you want to invest your life with. This will help you to form a clearer picture and get a better understanding of what is occurring within your relationships, enabling you to evaluate and decipher if they are meaningful or need to be reconsidered.

This process will also naturally cause you to consider the contributions you are making to the relationship. You can ask yourself if you are being respectful, responsible, and pleasant to be around (Dawson, 1994) and, if not, why? It will hold you accountable for your interactions and prompt you to be a better friend, partner, or family member. Collage used in this way helps to improve the quality of your relationship, make plans for changes, or identify evidence that it is time to move on.

Scott Neff, *Post Modern Temper*, 2020, Collage, Doug + Laurie Kanyer Art Collection

GEM 82 ▷ **Collage Sets Boundaries**

There are many reasons why you might find it difficult to set boundaries and say no to others. Maybe there's someone who won't take no for an answer or ignores the boundaries you set. Or maybe you do not want others to be upset, so you aim to please them more than advocate for yourself. It is vital to know you can learn, at any age, how to set boundaries in order to have your limits heard and respected. It is critical to know having your boundaries honored is one indication of a healthy and productive relationship.

You can make a collage finding words and elements to represent your "no" and develop ideas about how you can stand up for yourself by setting limits. You can include ideas in your collage about how to approach the issue with someone. One way to do this is to search your source material for a series of the word no and build a fence in your collage constructed of these no words.

A boundary-setting conversation can be tough, but your collage will give you new insights, and perhaps visual courage, to have the conversation. Once you've had the conversation and the boundaries are clear, your collage will be a continuous affirmation that you can establish healthy boundaries. You've done it before, and you can continue into the future. If you find your boundaries are not respected after the conversation, your collage will serve as proof of all your efforts to work on a healthy relationship. It will remind you that you can choose to make plans to remove yourself from situations where others are not respecting your "no."

GEM 83 ▷ **Collage Challenges Mind-Reading**

In order to deal with a multitude of experiences, you may use a shortcut as a way to cope. You might use mind-reading to predict the intent, thoughts, motivation, and outcomes of an interaction with others (Burns, 1980). Through patterns of observing others, you may have developed a bank of common assumptions about what others are thinking.

This pattern of thinking is developed in childhood, or another time in which you survived unpredictable circumstances. People, when faced with complex or threatening life circumstances, will cope by imagining they have the ability to read others' minds and predict their responses. This cognitive process, called negativity bias, is a creative way of coping with distressing events (Rozin & Royzman, 2001). You can begin to move from mind-reading others to being in the here and now. Each time you converse with others in your life, aim to discover what it is they really think and feel about what is taking place.

You might be tempted to bring forth those assumptions—mind-reading others—to balance yourself in the midst of a disorienting discussion full of unknowns. While mind-reading may serve to protect, it can also be unhelpful in forming relationships. When used in excess, mind-reading can stifle relationships and increase anxiety when you discover that your perception was mistaken.

To hold yourself accountable, use collage any time you find yourself saying, I know exactly what they are thinking. You can make a collage to discover if your mind-reading notions are true. You can illustrate others perceived thinking patterns in your collage and then take a step back to observe how they appear in physical form. When making your collage in this way you can ask yourself, what is the evidence for this conclusion? You can furthermore challenge yourself by inquiring, how do I know for sure that the person is thinking that? In this transformation of your thinking, you are asking yourself—is it true, is it helpful—while confronting you limiting patterns of mind-reading.

Dennis Busch, *Any Way the Wind Blows*, 2019, Collage, Doug + Laurie Kanyer Art Collection

GEM 84 ▷ **Collage Challenges All-or-Nothing Thinking**

To cope with the variance in others' behavior or to simplify a complex situation, you may be tempted to use all-or-nothing thinking (Burns, 1980). People do this to balance and calm themselves when faced with a large dose of conflicting information or perplexing behaviors. As you grew, you may have experienced people who acted delightful at times and then possibly disturbing other times. This is confusing to our nervous systems, which thrives on a sense of predictability. Over time and with experience, you may have come to understand the subtle things that influence others' behaviors. Perhaps you developed a comprehension that people are not always one way or the other. You saw the subtle nuances in people and situations and were able to see more than one side of things—seeing things in shades of grey.

From time to time, in the face of strain, you might recycle the trend towards all-or-nothing thinking. This defense mechanism can limit your relationships and appreciation of others. Certainly, there are times when you need to set a boundary with someone and make judgments based on conclusive evidence you have gathered. You may need to limit or halt interactions based on your experiences. But moving through the world categorizing others can be unfair and possibly block your human need for connection.

Make a collage to track what you have come to believe about others. See if, in fact, you have ample support to make a judgment using all-or-nothing thinking (Perhaps ask yourself, how do I know for sure that this person is bad or good, wrong or right, etc?). More times than not, what you observe is a signal to offer support, compassion, and context about what they are experiencing.

HollyAnna DeCoteau Littlebull, *I Am the Land, I Am the Water*, 2021, Collage, Doug + Laurie Kanyer Art Collection

Dana Caldera, *Space Between the Branches*, 2019, Collage, Doug + Laurie Kanyer Art Collection

Sarah Cowling, *Please Yourself First*, 2019, Collage and Paint on Canvas, Doug + Laurie Kanyer Art Collection

Gems Revealing Behind-the-Scenes

"Things aren't always what they seem
You're only seeing part of me
There's more than you could ever know
Behind the scenes."

—Francesca Battistelli
(Lyrics from the song *Behind the Scenes*)

GEM 85 ▷ **Collage Highlights the Value of Layers**

Are you familiar with the word strata? It refers to the layers of rock and sediment in the ground, deposited over time. If you were to slice into the ground like a piece of cake, you would see these layers. They are quite stunning, often of varied color, texture, and materials. When you observe strata, you observe a geological history of ancient foundations.

The history of your life functions much the same way. It comprises many layers of experiences and meaning. The process of layering involved in collage is a reflection of the layering of life experiences. There is a collage technique called decollage, where you glue layers upon layers of material to a foundation or substrate. Decollage is French, meaning to take off, and this manner of collage requires you to eventually cut, tear, slice, pick, or rip away pieces of the original image to reveal the layers behind the layers.

The layers build up to create magnificent depth and texture. The surface is usually bumpy and often visually complex, much like your life. As you build a collage with this method and the layers build, you will be able to have a visual representation of the various layered experiences in your life and reveal what is occurring behind the scenes.

Decollage's symbolic representation calls on you to become an artful archeologist. You might choose a tool, a dull knife, tweezers, or even your fingers. Once the glue sets, you can dig into the collage's surface and begin unearthing the layers! As you dig, you will see the under layers you glued down, and you can imagine the layers of your own life, too. Seeing the layers of paper and other materials peeled away as you artfully become an archeologist will give you the courage to dig deeper into your own life and explore what your life has been all about.

GEM 86 ▷ **Collage Shows Behind-the-Scenes**

Much like the unnoticed or unseen activities behind the curtain of a play, influencing what you see on stage, there are behind-the-scenes things happening in life experiences. They are the stories behind the stories, some hard and discouraging, others sweet and maybe even silly. Making a collage will offer you a symbolic way to think about some of the behind-the-scenes events of your life. You know they are there, influencing and impacting your life story. Making collages will give you a way to look behind the curtain to better understand the bigger picture of your life experiences.

Depending on how you construct your collage, you may choose to depict the on stage and behind-the-scenes narrative by collaging on both the front and back of your substrate. There may be an impressive difference between the front and the back. In many ways, this is like life itself—what you see right in front of you and what is happening behind-the-scenes. Examining the differences between the front and the back of the collage will help you to integrate this truth of life and invite inquiry about the reality of what you see and what you don't.

GEM 87 ▷ **Collage Addresses Thoughts of Persecution**

When you are not feeling settled emotionally, and relationships have been challenging, you can begin to feel a bit persecuted. Maybe you have had real hardships in the past where others have sought to undo you or maybe this is a new feeling that borders on irrational. Having thoughts that are colored with paranoia are most commonly linked to past experiences of dramatic vulnerability or real threats. When this happens you can have obsessive thoughts that intrude your awareness. You might feel behind-the-scenes others are working to disgrace, humiliate, or discredit you, or that something heavy is about to happen.

Laurie Kanyer, *Women and Dogs 1*, 2019, Collage, Doug + Laurie Kanyer Art Collection

In times like this it is vital to get a clearer viewpoint to clarify what you are thinking. Collage can help to reveal what is true and what needs to be attended to so you can decrease the isolation connected to these fears and build trust with yourself and others.

Make collages to track what you think is taking place behind-the-scenes. Challenge your thinking by using the back of the collage to document, with elements or in writing, the evidence that something devastating is going to happen. Make a commitment to yourself to talk to someone you trust about what you are thinking. The value of collage in this instance is it is relaxing (vital to healing when feeling persecuted), helps to release pleasure hormones, and the images you put on the collage can visually challenge, confirm, or clarify your thoughts. Those you share your collage with will be able to help you process and get assistance, if you need more help.

GEM 88 ▷ **Collage Depicts a Cumulative Effect**

All the events and situations in daily life can have a cumulative effect on your well-being. The cumulative effect of life is like a ball of yarn where you can see only the top layer of the yarn on the ball, but you know there are yards of yarn wound beneath, hidden from view. Over time, the mass accumulation of day-to-day events and pressures can become tiring, straining, and hard. It can be difficult to see the bigger picture.

When you make a collage, adding layer upon layer, you are actually witnessing this cumulative process in action. In seeing your collages and all the various layers, you will be able to have a broader visual of your experiences, offering you self-compassion and helping you to better understand and appreciate what you have gone through. You will gain a deeper appreciation for what you have sustained in life, and this will invite and instill empathy for yourself. When you observe your collage and all the layers, you may be able to say to yourself, now I see why I feel this way. My goodness, I have been through a lot in life.

GEM 89 ▷ **Collage Confirms What is True**

Have you had a sneaking feeling that your perceptions are more accurate than you are given credit for? Maybe someone frequently told you that your perception was wrong or what you knew to be true was not accurate. In times like this, you can make a collage to cross-reference what you know with what you've been told. You can then connect with others and confirm the accuracy of what you know to be true and reconsider things. You may be interacting with others who attempt to make you doubt yourself or events that you experienced. It's important to keep in mind that it is okay to effectively express yourself and have a conversation with these actors when they behave this way.

You can use collage to identify what you know to be true. You then can discuss your truth with others in order to clarify and hold each of you accountable for what you recall. If you feel your perspective and recollection have been discounted, take time to ponder on the perspective of others and make another collage with the new information. Know that, over time, more information may rise up for you to consider. Make sure to ponder and observe if you are being gaslit. By definition, this means the person intentionally changes the truth to control or manipulate you. Deeply considering your perspective by making a collage will allow you to gain confidence in what you know to be true, claim the power of that truth, and keep the lines of communication sharp and clear.

Lisa Myers Bulmash, *Safe-Not Safe Pt Gamble*, Collage, Doug + Laurie Kanyer Art Collection

GEM 90 ▷ **Collage Helps You to Confront Bullies and Oppressors**

When faced with a difficult person or a bully in your life, you can use collage to practice how you wish to deal with the situation. Making a collage about the situation will offer your internal wisdom a way to provide you with information about your true thoughts, feelings, and experiences connected to this person. Various sources of research indicate that some people demonstrating narcissistic or antisocial personality traits may aim to mistreat or harm others (Cloninger & Svrakic, 2008; Lowenstein, Purvis & Rose, 2016). Sadly, in some cases, traits they exibit have been developed over time after surviving complex trauma. They are often re-enacting what they survived (Trippany, Helm & Simpson, 2006).

If you believe you are a part of this abusive cycle, whether on the giving or receiving end, there are resources for you to find help. Nobody needs to hurt another person in order to have their needs met. You can always do some research to find the various resources available to you and learn ways to make healthy decisions about people who aim to unsettle your life.

Making a collage about potential methods to manage or leave these relationships will reinforce your knowledge, offering you a safe, confidential way to practice and prepare for the decisions you make.

Della Wells, *Him Again*, 2019, Collage, Doug + Laurie Kanyer Art Collection

Bonnie Denver Ruttan, *Bombard*, 2019, Collage, Doug + Laurie Kanyer Art Collection

Terry Ringler aka Trash Riot, *58*, 2020, Digital Collage, Doug + Laurie Kanyer Art Collection

Gems Refining Communication

"Communication is the fuel that keeps the fire of your relationships burning, without it, your relationship goes cold."

—William Paisley

GEM 91 ▷ Collage Uses Your First Language of Sight

Collage mirrors the way you first came to understand the world using your eyes. If you were born with sight, the first way you learned was through the portal of your eyes, which gave you knowledge of what your body was experiencing. While you made observations visually, you catalogued what you learned in the mental file drawers of your memories.

All the things you observed and experienced became bits of knowledge about the world around you. As your caregivers interacted with you using the spoken language of your people, they assigned the verbal labels, words, for the things you saw and experienced. Your ability to see came before your knowledge of spoken language; even in the womb you saw your environment.

When you use collage to explore feelings and life events, you are using your first language of seeing. When you choose elements—readymade images infused with established meaning—to tell your story, it is a quicker and more efficient way than using spoken, or even written words.

Using collage decreases the feeling of being overwhelmed by the situation, as you are using your first and most natural language to get to the matters at hand.

For the listener, sharing your collage provides visual images that actually intercepts the listener's natural need to formulate or conjure up an image in their own brain. They don't have to search for an image to relate your story to their own memory bank in order to comprehend the details when hearing your story. Collage allows for the use of a universally recognized picture proving more efficient and clear communication between everyone. A picture is worth a thousand words.

GEM 92 ▷ Collage Uses Your Sight to Insure Accurate Understandings

From the beginning of humankind, our eyes have been an exquisite tool that helps us to accurately interpret the world around us. Two people who are experiencing an event—seeing what is taking place—will more likely have the same, if not similar, impressions; versus information received by hearing. You and others understand best with your eyes first and foremost.

Have you ever played that game called gossip? People gather in a circle and one starts the game by telling the person next to them some piece of information or a short story. By the time the information is passed from one person to the next, and reaches the last person in the circle, it changes drastically. The initial message has been altered in the repeated telling. Often the original message is lost.

In using your collage you utilize a more accurate method to get your point across, the use of one's eyes to communicate rather than the ears. Images seen are much clearer than spoken, or even written words, as demonstrated by the gossip game. Words spoken and written can have a multitude of potential meanings and require the listener to do more work to understand. They have to, in the listening, work harder to see the message and may actually hear it inaccurately in the process.

Claire Standish, *Feathers*, 2017, Collage, Doug + Laurie Kanyer Art Collection

GEM 93 ▷ **Collage Fosters a Universally Understood Language**

The elements you cut out to make a collage are ready-made images infused with established meaning, and they act as universally understood symbols. Regardless of one's culture, race or language, the image of a hand is universally understood as a hand, a leg is a leg, and an eye is an eye. For this reason, collage offers you a chance to explore, mine, and resolve a theme, topic, event, or situation more easily. It allows for more clear and efficient communication between you and others. Additionally, as the first viewer of the collage you benefit dramatically. Collage gives you a deeper understanding of your thoughts and feelings, leading to a more effective pattern of communication and problem-solving, while improving your overall well-being.

GEM 94 ▷ **Collage Plans for Important Conversations**

Have you ever finished a key conversation and then noticed a flood of things you wish you had said? You might think, it's too late. You reflect and remember a number of key points. Too often, people go into an important conversation having little (if any) preparation. When that happens, you might have regrets, and the lines of communication may not be as brilliant as they could have been. You can transform a meeting or conversation pertaining to a relationship or important project that deserves your attention by preparing a thoughtful collage beforehand. You can choose elements to represent all the key points you want to make, which will help you to order your thoughts beforehand and enable you to clearly communicate your points to the other person. You can follow up once you have completed your collage and make notes if you want.

Essentially, in making a collage, you are employing your body—your hands, eyes, and the overall creative imagination of your brain—to elicit ideas and help you to remember what you want to say. The act of gluing will help you cement the notions you aim to bring forth. It is as though you are doing a rehearsal for an important real life play.

The bonus is that you can illustrate on the collage how you hope the conversation will turn out. You can place elements to show that you have respect for the other person. You can also place elements to show you are living your values and character traits. Making a collage affords you the opportunity to role play and practice the conversation beforehand. You can even move the cut-out elements around on the collage before you glue them.

In collage, all the details of your key points remain confidential. You might place the collage inside a folder to take with you to the meeting, glance at it during the conversation, or take a photo on your phone and have the photo cued up to look at during the talk. This visual aid can give you confidence and remind you of points you want to make.

Zach Collins, *Frugal*, 2020, Collage, Doug + Laurie Kanyer Art Collection

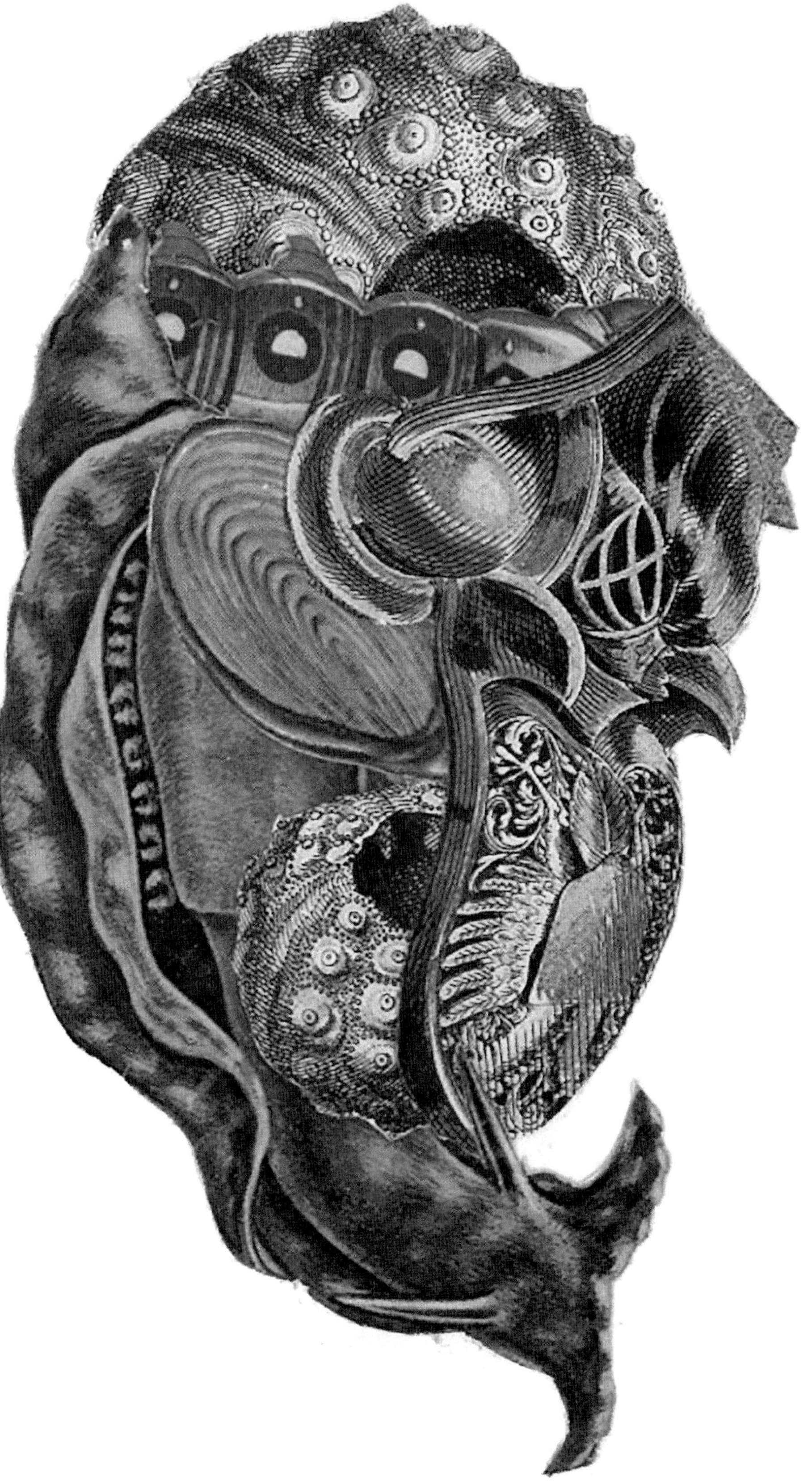

Stephen Payne, *Monster*, 2020, Collage, Doug + Laurie Kanyer Art Collection

Fred Free, *often a surprise*, 2019, Collage, Doug + Laurie Kanyer Art Collection

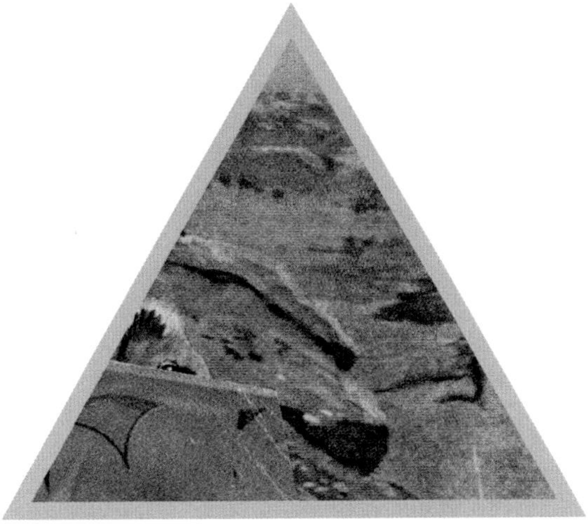

Gems Clarifying Beliefs, Causes & Values

"What lies behind us and what lies before us
are tiny matters compared to
what lies within us".

—Ralph Waldo Emerson

GEM 95 ▷ **Collage Clarifies Your Beliefs**

In searching for elements for your collage, you will come across interviews, essays, and other writings that express beliefs and values of others. You will find information you agree with and disagree with, giving you the opportunity to consider outside views and compare and contrast them with your own. This process allows you to define and fortify your beliefs and values, helping to advance them, inspiring you to seek more information.

GEM 96 ▷ **Collage Shows Your View Point**

Being clear about what you believe and expressing your values and opinions is vital to your emotional well-being. To fortify your beliefs, you may need a time of reflection—time to consider, research, and ponder what you value to be true and important to you. In fact, it is a wise thing to do, to really be able to articulate your values with intention and thoughtful responsibility.

Collage is a way to sort out your beliefs, to take the time to study and to contemplate. When you make a collage, you can show your point of view about a situation or topic. You can make collages about your political, social, and spiritual beliefs, giving you a chance to communicate your ideas and opinions at the same time. In this case, the old adage, let me show you what I think applies.

GEM 97 ▷ **Collage Reframes and Considers Others' Points of View**

When you make a collage about a situation, you have the ability to consider other ideas and look at the circumstances from a different perspective. In the same way you can make a collage about your ideas and opinions, you can make a collage about another person's point of view. This allows you a chance to gain a better understanding of their ideas. It also makes it possible to cross-reference your own point of view with theirs. In doing so, you have the opportunity to see and understand things in new and different ways, which expands both your understanding of self and another person's beliefs and values.

GEM 98 ▷ **Collage Allows for a Do-Over—Making Apologies for Conversations You Regret**

No matter who you are, you will experience conversations that leave you feeling horrible. They are a part of life. You can find yourself several days later shaking your head, wondering what happened, and what to do next. Likely, you believe relationships are so important you don't want to risk any breakdown in communication.

When you have a situation or conversation that did not go well, make a collage about it and practice communication skills for a revised do-over conversation. You can put all the details of what you said, heard, and regretted alongside what you wish you had said and heard. This will give you both a better understanding of what happened and a clear idea of how you wish to communicate in a do-over conversation. If you need to make an apology, you can practice making an apology on your collage, acknowledging the things you did that may have added more hurt upon hurt.

From there, you can ask the other person for an opportunity to have a new discussion. This will serve to strengthen your communication skills and dissolve the potency of residual feelings left from a negative conversation.

Rosie Schinners, *Sanctuary*, 2019, Collage and watercolor, Doug + Laurie Kanyer Art Collection

GEM 99 ▷ **Collage as Protest**

Are you fed up and want to speak up? Collage has historical roots in protest. In her article, *Collage as a Process for Reclamation, Black Collage in Conversation with Teri Henderson*, Emily Owens wrote: "Beginning in the early 20th century with the Dada Movement, collage entered Western art history with political overtones, anti-war sentiments, and the breaking of long-established gender norms. Through the act of slicing photographic imagery from the media, artists were able to recontextualize popular imagery to suit their motivations" (Owens, 2021). Author Betty Quinn said, in reference to Hannah Höch "Dadaism (an art movement that used collage in the form they called photomontages) tapped into the trauma of a destabilized Europe (during WWI) reeling from the effects of the war. Photomontages in particular were a popular technique employed by Dadaists, clipping found images from mass media to create a setting that articulated the instability and anger of the world at the time. Photomontages were a form of revolution and protest" (Quinn, 2019).You can create a collage protest using the newspapers and magazines that feature stories of topics that elicit great concern and emotion. Make a collage slicing the images of political figures into absurd new beings, as the famous collagist Hannah Höch did, to voice your opinion and protest.

With collage, you do not have to go silent, bottling up your thoughts and emotions related to world events or people in positions of power. You can voice your sentiments and protest with images and words using collage.

Miloo (Emily Geirnaert), *SO FAR, SO CLOSE*, 2020, Collage, Doug + Laurie Kanyer Art Collection

Yannick Lowery, *Burn*, 2020, Collage, Doug + Laurie Kanyer Art Collection

Allan Bealy, *Seraph*, 2019, Collage, Doug + Laurie Kanyer Art Collection

Gems Inspiring Awe, Wonder & Beauty

"Without the emotion of the beautiful,
the sublime, the mysterious,
there is no art, no religion,
no literature."

—John Burroughs

GEM 100 ▷ **Collage Evokes Sublime Awe and Wonder**

The sublime is understood and defined to mean the quality of grandeur that inspires awe and wonder. This concept and the emotions it ignites have been a source of inspiration for artists throughout history. When you make a collage that strikes you deeply, filling you with awe and wonderment, you are touching the sublime. Awe is a special emotion and one that is important to experience, as it displaces feelings of disdain for the world. Awe leads you instead to a place of heightened feelings of spirituality and connectedness with the all-encompassing embrace of the universe. To behold the sublime is to expand beyond the mundane world and recognize the mystical grandeur of life. It is a feeling of profound wonder and wholehearted amazement.

When you make a collage that causes you to feel awestruck by what you see, you will experience a true emotional summit, creating a weighty and potent memory for you to recall in the future. Collage allows for unfolding. These types of emotionally potent, positive memories will sustain you in times of trial and tribulation in the future. Any time you need to evoke this awestruck emotion, you have the luxury of looking at your collage!

GEM 101 ▷ **Collage Inspires Beauty**

Beauty has profound power in your life. As Plato once said, "The contemplation of beauty causes the soul to grow wings." However, the beauty I am referring to is not a cultural construct or standard held by way of social conditioning. It is deeper than that—a feeling tone that inspires aspiration and deep passion, helping to uplift your soul.

As you make a collage, you will see many images that convey an idea of beauty and its subsequent social standards. This gives you an opportunity to compare and reflect on how you define beauty and what inspires it within you. In doing so, you affirm your individuality and strengthen your ability to discern between surface beauty and soulful beauty—to aspire and hold yourself to a more meaningful standard. It may be out of step with society; however, it is not only commendable, but it is also a healthy emotional and intellectual practice.

GEM 102 ▷ **Collage Shows the Mystery of Happenstance—Inspires Wonder**

When you make art, a marvelous wonder takes place—a little mystery—and this is especially true with collage. As you search for just the right elements and you're thinking about what it is you want to find, an element seems to magically appear as though that particular element was waiting for you. This sweet surprise supports your emotional well-being and brings forth joy. Some might call this coincidence, others might call it luck, but this happenstance of attraction feels as though the universe is listening in on your very thoughts.

With collage, there is often excitement and expectation to see what will magically come forth. In an interview on *The Takeaway* podcast, Tania Luna, the co-author of *Surprise: Embrace the Unpredictable and Engineer the Unexpected*, said the human brain goes through the "surprise sequence... It's a strong neurological alert that tells us that something is important about this moment and we have to pay attention" (Meinzer & Raphael, 2015, 1:09). Luna also suggested that feelings like happiness and joy are more common when we are surprised. In making a collage, you break the pattern of doldrums in your daily life, offering joyful surprises and igniting curious wonder and profound joy.

Luciana Frigerio, *Finding a Place of My Own*, 2019, 3D Collage, Doug + Laurie Kanyer Art Collection

GEM 103 ▷ **Collage Creates the Sacred**

There are things placed in your heart that you hold dear, in the very soul of your existence. Naturally, that which is considered holy, spiritual, or sacred will differ for each person. Whether it has occurred to you or not, you are an expression of the Divine. You were purely created to experience and express the holy in your own way.

Collagist Matt McCarthy dedicated his entire creative efforts to making collages of cats. His work might be considered a modern-day twist on the Egyptian deities. He holds them in seemingly sacred regard, even when the collages are silly. His art, no doubt means something sacred to him, and for cat lovers, they clearly resonate as profound. What you hold in high regard matters, and you can make sacred collages to represent your reverence for that which you love. You might choose to make a collage that has religious meaning. As in some cultures, you can choose to use your collage as the focal point of an altar or sacred space. Others may feel the same way and will benefit from seeing your most holy and sacred collage.

GEM 104 ▷ **Collage Shows the Curious Connections in Life**

Have you ever heard the expression opposites attract or observed people who are somehow connected but don't seem to fit together? So it is with collage—two seemingly polarized things coming together to form something that is pleasing and delightful.

As you make collages, you will choose elements from various unrelated sources. The subject matter of your source materials will likely have no logical connection to one another. Apart from each other, these elements may not appear to have any relationship; but, once put together on the collage, they seem a perfect fit. As you make selections for your collage and place disconnected elements together, it will ignite your curiosity and wonder—encouraging you to look beyond yourself and your life circumstances for new and interesting opportunities that you may not have considered.

GEM 105 ▷ **Collage Liberates and Offers Beneficial Spontaneity**

When faced with challenges, it is quite normal to freeze, to be paused, stuck and uncertain. It can be as if you are so flooded with confusion you become an unmovable statue, arrested in place, unsure of what to do. This response can overwhelm your functioning as you sink into bewilderment. You may struggle to determine what move to make, which can contribute to feeling more stuck or devastated. Maybe you are cautious by nature, which can require more time to make decisions. You may struggle to know how to proceed, which, over the years, can manifest in anxiety and procrastination. Part of you wants to make a move, but you are held back. Collage can help to remove the logjam of confusion and let water pass through toward a solution. The act of making a collage, with or without a specific intention, will begin to impact and activate the parts of the brain that unleash problem-solving.

Dopamine, a key neurotransmitter in your brain's reward circuitry, may contribute to a new feeling of hope. Slowly, as you make your collage, you will become more spontaneous. You will free up the clogged drain caused by the slog of either your initial response to a situation or a lifetime of anxious caution. This creative process symbolically gives you permission to thaw your frozen stance. Permission is the first step in the expression of feeling and problem-solving (Brackett, 2019). Giving yourself permission is similar to the green light of go you get when driving. Permission is the freeing magic sauce leading to new discoveries and insight on feelings. With collage, which has no rules, you are free. Once you give yourself permission to move spontaneously and remove the chains of uncertainty, you are able to live as you need. Collage will loosen your defenses and allow you to emerge into a new existence.

Brian Barker, *Quarantine Dreams 3*, 2020, Collage,
Doug + Laurie Kanyer Art Collection

Brian Barker, *Quarantine Dreams 4*, 2020, Collage,
Doug + Laurie Kanyer Art Collection

Rebeka Elizegi, *MIX1*, 2020, Collage,
Doug + Laurie Kanyer Art Collection | Portrait Photo by Mar C. Llop

Rebeka Elizegi, *MIX2*, 2020, Collage,
Doug + Laurie Kanyer Art Collection | Portrait Photo by Mar C. Llop

Miguel Ontiveros, *Border Crossing*, 2018, Collage, Doug + Laurie Kanyer Art Collection

Gems Comforting Heavy Events, Grief, & Loss

"Anything that's human is mentionable, and anything that is mentionable can be more manageable. When we can talk about our feelings, they become less overwhelming, less upsetting, and less scary. The people we trust with that important talk can help us know that we are not alone."

—Fred Rogers

GEM 106 ▷ **Collage Illustrates What is Too Difficult to Speak**

Likely, as many people do, you will experience something so heavy or so horrible that you deem it unspeakable. Collage offers you a chance to show and tell others about a life experience that is too heavy to put into words. You can make a simple or complex collage to illustrate it without the need for words. The collage will become your voice. It can tell the story. You will be liberated and freed when the event causes you to not know what to say.

Heavy life events need to be revealed to reduce the power they hold on your life. The strain of keeping them to yourself is not only hard on your mental processes, but on your entire body. In the movie *Labyrinth*, Sarah, the protagonist played by actress Jennifer Connelly, comes face to face with her antagonist Jareth, played by David Bowie. After spending some time fighting with Jareth and his arduous tests within the labyrinth to rescue her baby brother, Sarah has a moment of reflection. She looks Jareth in the eye and calmly says, "You have no power over me," which returns Jareth to a container, a crystal ball. She saw the truth and found the words to speak truth to Jareth's perceived power.

You deserve to exclaim these words in the face of your hardships. Your collage can help you to do so. In fact, you could cut those words out, "You have no power over me," and add them to the collage! When you choose elements representing the aspects of the hardship, the things you're grappling with, the resulting collage will reveal insights. Thus, the collage allows you to visually communicate when it's otherwise too difficult to find the words. And the truth—you are technically not speaking the horrible truth—you are showing it! The collage becomes your voice to out the onerous event and rid yourself of the power it has over you! Making a collage will offer you the time and space to practice telling, while you gently discover the words to speak the event with your voice.

GEM 107 ▷ **Collage Illustrates Disaster or Loss**

Experiencing a disaster or loss can sometimes be too much to wrap the mind around and perhaps too hard to accept. In these cases, the brain must work especially hard to insert the experience into your life narrative. The shock, denial, and associated grief can be so intense that the experience is temporarily suspended as true. In particular, this profound form of denial comes when the experience is sudden, unexpected, and dramatic.

People use denial and avoidance to shield themselves from the pain of what they experienced and some may believe talking about it will only increase suffering. They believe that focusing on other things and avoiding conversation will contain the event and minimizes the loss' effect. However, what those of us in the helping professions know is that healing comes when people share and others are present to hear about our sorrows.

While denial is a stage naturally people go through, it can confuse and disrupt life immensely. Making a collage about an unbelievable experience serves to illustrate—slowly and respectfully—what occurred. It will help clear up misunderstandings, potentially reveal more information, and make visible the event's impact. Your collage will act as proof and help you accept the event as factual and real. Creating a symbolic visual representation will allow the brain to incorporate the experience in the overall understanding of your personal life history.

Jessica Whittingham, *Bless this Home*, 2020, Collage, Doug + Laurie Kanyer Art Collection

GEM 108 ▷ **Collage Illustrates Pain—Helps Others Understand**

Emotional pain is invisible to others, unlike a physical injury, which is easier to see and observe. No wonder others have a difficult time extending compassion and empathy when you are hurting emotionally. Others simply can't see the depth of your suffering. Really, unless those in your life are experiencing the same exact situation, or have had a similar event in their life as a reference point, it can be hard for you to find true empathy.

When the pain is intense, and others can't easily observe it, seeming to go on about their business, forgetting how much you hurt—it can add more pain to what you are going through. This pain, and the lack of compassion, can be so heavy you may want to find other ways to show your pain or you may be seeking other sources of pain instead, something other than what you are currently feeling. You may be desperate to find anything to distract you from the heavy thoughts.

Without a way to show the pain, to get relief, you may feel like turning to self-destructive, harmful behaviors—alternative coping techniques to defer pain and to show others the depth of your hurt. While an alternative, they are often not effective or restorative.

A definition for these actions is short-term energy-relieving behaviors, or STERBs. A STERB is any behavior designed to defer the depth of pain by offering temporary distraction. STERBs rarely lead to recovery from pain or solve the origin of the pain. STERBs like binge drinking, overeating, gambling, excessive spending, over exercising, compulsive sexual behaviors or self harm by cutting, can actually create additional adversity. New challenges like chemical dependency, unexpected re-traumatization, shame, or relationship strain can develop when a STERB is used. The STERB may offer short-term diversion, but STERBs do not bring you closer to resolution of the initial pain and can complicate it (Ferentz, 2014). STERBs are non-verbal expressions of needs and collage is a healthier and productive alternative when facing deep pain.

Making a collage offers you a safe way to express and show your intense feelings of pain instead of hurting yourself by using a STERB. Making a collage offers you a cathartic outlet; in the process, you create a vessel in which to place and contain your pain. It will give you something to show others so they can understand how much you hurt. Making a collage about the event(s) causing the emotional strain will allow for a safe, healthy release of heavy emotions. You can also choose to show it to others to help them to see how you feel so they can support and care for you.

GEM 109 ▷ **Collage Shows You Can Put Things Back Together**

Life is a cycle of beginnings and endings, of creation and destruction. Sometimes the destruction comes without invitation or warning. This can cause a range of emotions and prompt the limbic system to act (the fight, flight, or freeze part of your brain), which seeks safety, control and protection. Change can be overwhelming, especially when a large, unanticipated life alterations come forth.

You can comfort yourself when experiencing dramatic—invited or uninvited—change by making a collage to symbolically put things back in an order you need or maybe reconfigure a new order to ease the discomfort. With collage making you can choose elements to show all the aspects of the disruption or change, too. In doing so, it will represent your effort to endure during upheaval, showing your ability to seek balance during the hardships, and give you a focal point for where life is today. The collage you make can give you a chance to express your thoughts and feelings about what is taking place so you don't have to be silent. This act of building the collage will help to restore a feeling of control, predictability, and certainty.

David Crunelle, *Her Conditional Embrace*, 2020, Collage, Doug + Laurie Kanyer Art Collection

GEM 110 ▷ **Collage Illustrates Wholeness and Restoration**

During times of emotional upheaval, you might feel like you are coming apart at the seams, as though you are disconnected from yourself and your body. There are a couple of ways people experience this phenomena of being disconnected.

One way is, that little inner voice in your head creates a pattern of focusing on the scattered elements of the upheaval. It may say to you, I am coming apart at the seams or my life is a disaster. This pattern of self-talk can become a frame for how you see your life and can reinforce feelings of being scattered and broken, rather than seeing other aspects that are going well.

Another way you may experience times of heavy emotional upheaval is commonly called dissociation, where the brain, in the face of immense hardship, will disconnect to manage and protect you from the intensity of the situation. Dissociation is a spectrum of experiences that often precede unhelpful STERBs, too. It can be a temporary or extended event, where you feel as though your life is not real (derealization), feel like you're hovering outside your life, watching it like a movie (depersonalization), or are numb to your physical sensations (analgesia), instead of experiencing it (Ferentz, 2014). Most people will have times of dissociation in their lifetime in response to an overwhelming experience or event. It is understandable that the brain, under undue strain, will seek ways to decrease the heaviness of the situation.

For both self-talk struggles and dissociation, making a collage can be a way to compare and contrast one's life, to see the depth of hardship and to center yourself when in a period of temporary disconnect. You can confront your negative self-talk in your collage and you can ground yourself to move through the period of dissociation using collage.

When you make a collage, you have a visual representation in bits and pieces of how you may be feeling. As you glue the elements down to the substrate, you are symbolically putting things back together and helping to dissolve your feelings of brokenness.

When you feel as though you are floating above yourself in a period of dissociation, you can observe—actually witness—yourself making the collage, watching your hands hold a magazine and cutting the element out for the collage. This will invite you to move back into the here and now, as opposed to floating outside your awareness. When you complete your collage, you see something that is together and whole. You are then invited to integrate the event as part of your world. At times of emotional upheaval, this will remind you of your strengths in coping and prove to you that you are complete and whole.

GEM 111 ▷ **Collage Helps with the Initial Impact of Grief**

Collage is an amazing way to cope with the initial grief experience. When you first encounter a remarkable loss, you may feel as though you are in an altered state of awareness. As the brain adjusts to the loss it has to do intense rearranging of experiences and memories to make room for this new information. This is often described as a feeling, by people experiencing loss, as being suspended in another world.

Collage will help to ground you as you respond to the loss and move the potent flood of horomones through the body, affording you some relief and comfort.

Jay Berrones, *A Rest is a Note Too*, 2016, Collage, Doug + Laurie Kanyer Art Collection

GEM 112 ▷ **Collage Proves You are Alive When There Has Been a Significant Loss**

You understand who you are, and the order of your world, in the context of who and what is in your life on an on-going basis. The predictable interactions you have with others and your environment each and every day helps to shape your understanding of your reality. The regular interactions with others grounds you, offers a feeling of security, and contributes to your identity—who you see yourself to be. When a loss takes place and those you are connected with are gone, it causes a dramatic interruption in the regular patterning you have come to know and forces you, often without your permission, to examine your identity and world.

Naturally, this can cause a profound fissure in the foundation of your world. Sometimes the fissure is so deep that you may not feel as though you are alive due to possible dissociation, which can be like an altered state of awareness. When you make a collage, you are witnessing yourself in the process. You see your hands as they cut the paper and glue down your elements. You experience and witness your own existence as you make a collage. During a time of loss, collage shows you exist when you do not feel as though you can even breathe.

Once completed, the resulting collage acts as a visual testament, proof to you that you exist, as you are now working to merge this new, most heavy loss into how you see yourself and understand the world around you.

GEM 113 ▷ **Collage Supports the Expression of the Stages of Grief**

If you are grieving a loss, collage is an excellent tool to help you experience the stages of grief, which are uniquely articulated by each individual and are not always experienced in sequential order. In her book *On Death and Dying*, Elizabeth Kübler-Ross documented five stages of grief (Kübler-Ross, 1969). Recently, her long-time associate David Kessler published *Finding Meaning: The Sixth Stage of Grief* (Kessler, 2019), adding a new stage called meaning.

One thing to consider is that the Kübler-Ross model was created for people dealing with the reality of their own death or terminal illness. Collage can be an effective way to apply meaning to traumatic loss, loss of agency, divorce, etc. without the pressure of documenting it a specific way.

Kübler-Ross's and Kessler's collective stages of grief:

Denial or shock - This can't really be happening to me!
Anger - Why did this happen to me?
Bargaining - I would do anything to trade places with the deceased.
Sadness - Sorrow and despair over the truth of the loss.
Acceptance - Integration of the loss as a true part of current life.
Making meaning - Not closure, but moving toward peace and hopefulness.

Using collage you can experience and document each stage of your grieving process in the order they present in your life. Collage will help you to identify and express what you may be feeling, alleviating the confused and disconnected feelings. It will allow you to better understand your loss and make meaning as you heal.

Rhed Fawell, *From Scotland With Love*, 2018, Collage, Doug + Laurie Kanyer Art Collection

GEM 114 ▷ **Collage Mirrors the Experience of Loss and Grief**

In many ways, the actions necessary in making a collage mirror the change, destruction, and devastation you experience when faced with a loss. As you make a collage, the pages you are using cease to exist in their original form. You are cutting and tearing the sheets of paper; as you do, you see the impact of the destruction, much like the way your own life has been torn apart. As you glue the elements to the substrate, you are replicating the work of constructing new chapters in your life due to the loss you endured. The collage shows your efforts to patchwork your life together in a new configuration as you grieve. The end result is like an additional chapter in your book of life, one full of sorrow. It is a visual statement, making some meaning of the loss, coming to an understanding of what you are living and its profound impact.

You can use collage-making as a way to experience and express the stages of grief you are going through. With each element you choose, you can show the experience. With each element you cut and place, you are doing the tasks of grieving, confronting denial, expressing anger, bargaining, sadness, acceptance, and making meaning. As you gaze upon the collage, both during the process of creation and upon completion, you have a visual rendering of the significant changes in your life.

Emotionally, making a collage offers you a chance to see the magnitude of what you are living. The collage process, especially when done over and over again during heavy change, supports you in supporting yourself. It can offer a way to have some predictability when life feels so uncertain. Making a collage tends to the wound of the loss by illustrating—showing the wounding. Additionally, making many collages in a time of deep grief will record your journey during this time of a most uninvited life event. You will be able to observe your life as you grieve while making collage, and this will support you in an unknown terrain. During a time of loss or change, this will help to affirm how you feel and what you are experiencing.

GEM 115 ▷ **Collage Helps Tell Secrets Without the Weight of Words**

Many of us carry secrets too heavy to share or to speak about with others. Holding on to them can compromise your emotional health. Oftentimes, those holding on to secrets do so because they have been threatened with harm if they tell. They also may believe no one will believe them.

Because of the solitary and confidential nature of collage, you can begin to share potent and heavy secrets, first with yourself and then with others if you choose. When you see and witness yourself making the collage, you observe yourself telling the secret, and this is powerful for you emotionally in healing the damage caused by keeping the secret.

Making a collage will give you a visual representation of the secret you carry, affirming that it really happened. It is right there in front of you and the truth of your secret can't be denied. In making a collage about a secret, you are able to tell your truth, gain personal power over the secret by getting it off your chest, and begin to take steps to improve the quality of your emotional well-being.

Madonna Mayfield, *Primavera I*, 2020, Collage, Doug + Laurie Kanyer Art Collection

Jeremiah Duncan, *Finding a Place of My Own*, 2019, Collage, Doug + Laurie Kanyer Art Collection

Gems Building Community & Belonging

"Giving connects two people, the giver and the receiver, and this connection gives birth to a new sense of belonging."

—Deepak Chopra

GEM 116 ▷ **Collage Grows Interdependence and Cooperation**

The very nature of collage is one of cooperation and interdependence. For example, someone who offered their time, skills, and talent originally created the content of the material you use to make your collage. Then, someone published the content and distributed it. There is also the person who no longer needed the material, so it has now come into your possession. Creating collage inherently requires the interdependence of other people. When you make a collage, even if working alone, there is always a cooperative connection between you and others through the materials you are using.

Collaborating on a collage is another way to foster connection with others while practicing cooperation. Each person involved begins a series of collages and trades them. The collages circulate between two artists. Each collagist adds their own elements to finish the collage. Each finished collage is an interdependant, cooperative effort by the two artists. The results will not only amaze you, they will be a beautiful visual reminder of the community you built together and give you a sense of connection and belonging. As collagist Greg Traw says, "Collage is a collaboration of people, context, meaning, and materials—all juxtaposed."

GEM 117 ▷ **Collage Humbles You**

When you see others' lives being shared in magazines, regarding sociological topics and current world events (we're thinking beyond fashion or entertainment here), you have an invitation to evaluate your situation and make comparisons. These comparisons may switch your current mindset, causing you to move out of yourself, and have compassion for the struggles of others. In this way, collage allows you to count your blessings. It helps to put things in a different perspective, taking the focus off of you and events in your life and redirecting it to something bigger than yourself. You may be moved to find a way to be of service to others, which will increase your connections with others and improve your emotional well-being, too.

GEM 118 ▷ **Collage Builds Belonging Through Sharing a Project**

Have you heard the folk story of Stone Soup? The narrator of the story has a soup pot and a single stone and then asks others to bring items to help make stone soup. People contribute potatoes, onions, carrots, and other ingredients. They eventually have enough to feed the whole community. It is a wonderful tale of how people can support one another and build community by sharing resources.

All over the world, the collage community has traditions similar to Stone Soup where people come together to share materials and make collages. Sometimes, collage makers contribute collage to be used in an exhibition. *The Collage Garden*, invented by Dutch artist and Norway resident Angela Gobbens (aka @miss.printed on Instagram) is one such effort. She identifies guest curators all over the world who facilitate an exhibition in their city. Then, via Instagram, she invites collagists all over the world to send garden-themed collages to be exhibited by a guest curator. Everyone is welcome to take part in this exhibition, and it builds a sense of belonging and inclusion. *The Collage Garden* has taken place in countries such as Spain, Norway, Nepal, The Netherlands, the United States, Russia, Scotland, France, and Italy.

You can take part in *The Collage Garden* or start a tradition amongst those you know of making Collage Stone Soup where each participant brings elements on an identified theme, building a massive collage mural on the theme. People will feel like an included part of the community, and the community will be elevated by making collage.

Charles Wilkin, *Lightening Strikes*, 2019, Collage, Doug + Laurie Kanyer Art Collection

GEM 119 ▷ **Collage Remembers Someone You Love**

Whether the person who inspires your collage is alive or deceased, making it can allow you to express your devotion for them. Like all emotions, they are felt, but their energy can't be actually seen, only witnessed by the effect they have on each person. Love, being one of the most potent emotions, is the source of artistic masterpieces, but what about those who have not learned the technical skill of painting? How can they show their love in a creative way? Making a collage can be your method to make a symbolic representation of your love.

Making a collage will help to fortify your sentiments of love and show others the deep feelings you have for another. Especially when away from the person you love for whatever reason, your collage will remind you of the intimacy and commitment of your relationship.

In the case where one you love, person or pet, is deceased, the collage of love offers a way to illustrate the relationship, which has changed significantly but is not over, as the feelings of deep love remain. The act of making a collage for the one you love will help you as you grieve and make a physical image to demonstrate the love you had while they were alive, which still goes on. You can use images of the actual items that belonged to the person you cherish—choose various photographs of them and even include personal items you have of theirs. Collage is a beautiful way to celebrate and commemorate your love and commitment to the people in your life who you revere and love.

GEM 120 ▷ **Collage Expresses Gratitude**

It is common knowledge that expressing gratitude is good for your mental health (Paquette, 2015). We know from neuroscience that when you express gratitude, the feel-good hormones dopamine and serotonin are immediately released into the system. Both are known to aid in mood enhancement and cause you to feel better. Being grateful moves you to a place of being a recipient, offering you an opportunity to account for the gifts of life.

When you consciously choose to be grateful, you are really saying thank you. Giving thanks causes you to become humble and offers you a chance to embrace your place in the grand scheme of life. Making a daily collage about things you are grateful for allows you to see the extraordinary opportunity you have to experience life itself.

One of the artists in the Doug + Laurie Kanyer Art Collection, Kiki Buccini, founded a collage movement she called Gift Collages. During the early days of the COVID-19 pandemic of 2020, she began to send out collages made on postcards. She hand inscribed inspirational quotes on the flip side of each postcard. She sent them to people she knew and strangers, too, including essential workers. Her goal was to express gratitude to those who were serving others in a time of global hardship. She recognized that even postal carriers would experience the joy of her collages as they delivered them!

Choosing to be grateful and making collage gifts challenges your mindset, inviting you to see the gift of being alive. This can help you to improve your emotional and mental state.

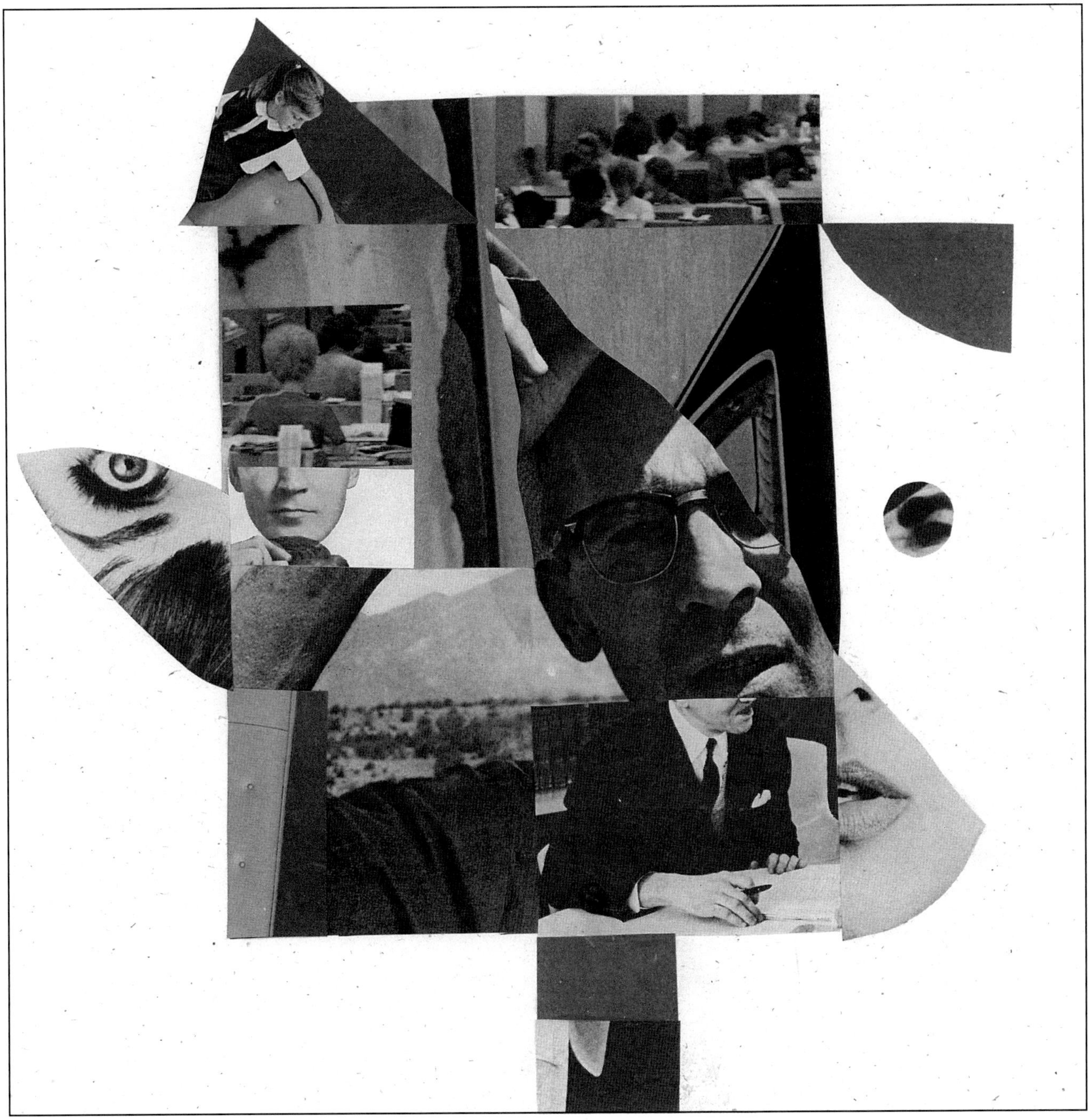

John Whitlock, *New York Times*, 2018, Doug + Laurie Kanyer Art Collection

GEM 121 ▷ **Collage Offers You a Way to Practice Giving**

Making a collage as a gift to others has powerful effects, improving your mood and strengthening your relationships (Paquette, 2015). Along with all the positive physiological effects, it deepens your relationship with the recipient and strengthens social ties. Making and giving a gift of collage helps the giver and the recipient to feel remembered, decreasing feelings of loneliness while increasing levels of social cooperation and belonging.

Making a collage for someone else fosters trust as you are showing that you are there and can be counted on. Making and giving a collage will ignite an explosion of gratitude in others. It is like a promise into the future that you will see each other again! As Queen Elizabeth said in a speech regarding the 2020 pandemic, "We will be with our friends again, we will be with our families again, we will meet again" (Dymond, 2020). Start a flood of loving, kindness, and connectedness by sending a gift of a collage and see how it transforms your emotions and relationships.

GEM 122 ▷ **Collage Takes Part in a Cause and Makes Contributions**

As you make collage, you are actually being socially responsible—taking part in something bigger than yourself. As you make collage, you are actively taking part in the cause of recycling, you are not stuck or helpless or non-productive. When you are going through a time of hardship, it can be life-giving to have things to contribute to, as this gives you new places to focus your attention and witness yourself making contributions.

It is quite amazing how in making collage (which uses discarded materials that could very well end up in a landfill) you are helping to preserve and care for the earth. You are making a contribution to the world at large. When you make collage, you are transforming these materials, otherwise seen as trash or useless, into something new, important and meaningful. It coincides with the value of being resourceful and supporting the preservation of the earth. Making collages can be your way of taking part in a cause and making a contribution, which can make you feel useful and connected to the the earth and its people. You are part of the solution of making a contribution to preserving the earth. And who knows what your next contribution will be? You can start with collage and move to other ways to make a difference in this world.

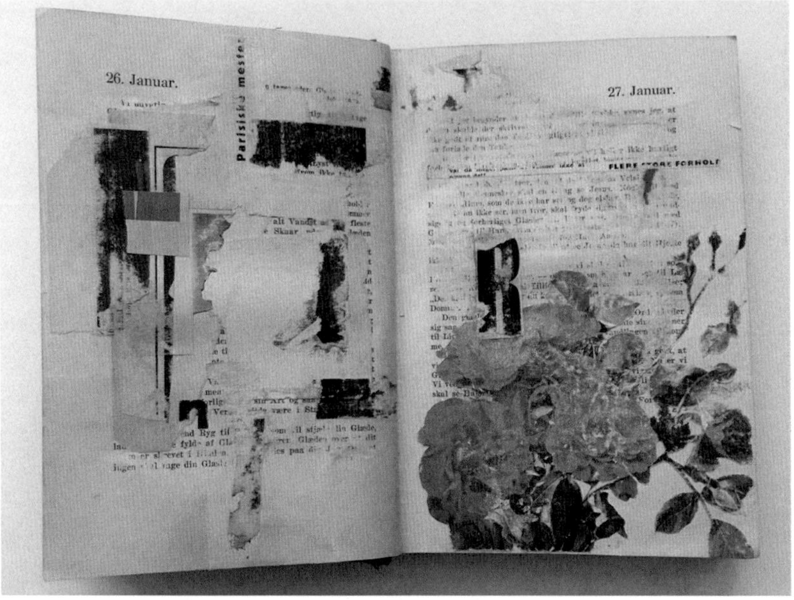

Anne Misfeldt, *Roses*, 2021, Collage on Sketchbook Page, Courtesy of the Artist

Kayla Lamotte, *Relatively Conscious*, 2020, Collage, Doug + Laurie Kanyer Art Collection

Camila Fernández, *Good Escape*, 2020, Digital Collage, Doug + Laurie Kanyer Art Collection

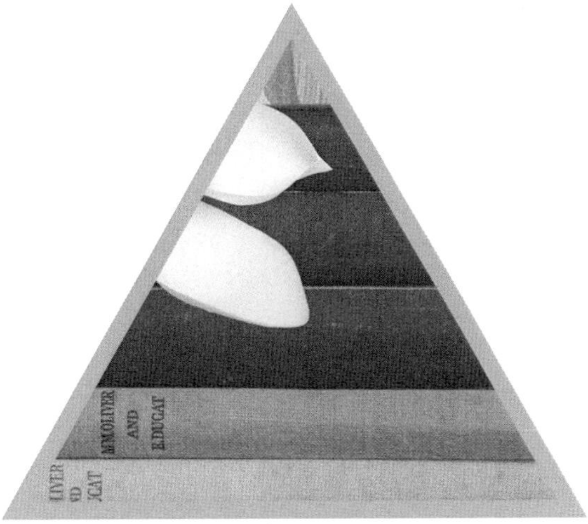

Gems Assisting Goal-Setting & Large Projects

"Far away there in the sunshine are my highest aspirations.
I may not reach them, but I can look up and see
their beauty, believe in them, and try
to follow where they lead."

—Louisa May Alcott

GEM 123 ▷ **Collage Sees Your Life Dreams and Inspires Hope to Achieve Them**

For your dreams to come true, it takes more than just optimistic imagining or positive thinking. It requires a willingness to put in the hard work and a strong sense of hope to keep you motivated. Making a collage about what you dream, using the elements of hope as your subject matter, will assist you in actualizing your ambitions.

Hope is a combination of will (your self-determination), plus commitment (a pledge to do something in the future), and motivation (deliberately engaging your inner drive to reach a great potential). The act of making a collage itself enlists the elements of hope and fortifies your resolve.

Consider how, in making a collage, you engage in a demonstration of hope by using your will (I am determined to make a collage), making a commitment (I will have this collage completed by Monday), and engaging your motivation (I am excited to see how all this hard work will create a finished collage). The collage-making itself helps you to practice the elements of hope!

Choosing to make a collage with symbols to illustrate the elements of hope—your will, commitment and motivation—will help to cement your ambitions deeply in your mind and provide you a visual image to reinforce your desires. In making a collage about your dreams, with the knowledge of the elements of hope, you move yourself from optimistic thinking to the physical act of creation.

Then you can go on to combine the power of optimism and positive thinking with the elements of hope on your collage, and you will have a dynamic visual representation to support the actualization of your goal. This act increases the likelihood of your dreams coming true. You move from holding your dream in your mind's eye to creating a physical object you can touch, to practicing steps of hope on the pathway to realizing your dreams.

GEM 124 ▷ **Collage Visually Reminds You of Your Heart's Desire**

You can make a collage to create a symbolic expression of your aspirations and goals. Recently, people have come to refer to these types of collages as vision boards. I prefer to call them Heart's Desire Collages™. What the eyes can see; the heart, mind, and soul can remember.

Making a visible piece of art—a collage to have in your immediate awareness— helps you to bring forth your dream. When you have a heart's desire, you hold that goal symbolically in the chambers of your heart and soul, attaching your heartstrings to the aspiration. There are actual strings in your heart called *chordae tendineae*, which do the work to open and close valves, pumping blood throughout your body. When you make a Heart's Desire Collage, it's as though you are tugging on the strings of your heart to help you do the work of bringing the goal into reality.

The collage you make about a dream or goal you have invites you to engage your heart strings, and captivates the motivation you will need to do the work, while inspiring you to take the necessary steps. The collage visually reserves a space in your consciousness for the dream to take hold and amplify. A Heart's Desire Collage helps to magnify the goal as a priority in your mind's eye, planting it deeply as a seed of passion in your heart. When you keep it visible in your immediate surroundings, you are viewing a commitment—the promise made to yourself—and a constant reminder to fortify the hopes you have for the future. In doing so, you engage your will in achieving your goals.

This is not magic, although it can seem like it! Rather, it is a powerful tool to help you create the reality you so desire. It is important to note here that your Heart's Desire Collage acts as step one in the actualization of a goal. Without taking the second step of doing the actual work, the chances of your dreams coming true become much slimmer.

Sara Vattano, *I sing*, 2020, Digital Collage, Doug + Laurier Kanyer Art Collection

GEM 125 ▷ **Collage Assists in Project Planning and Goal Actualization**

In order to accomplish a large project, it is helpful to be able to see the big picture and all the small details before you begin. In the same way architects make scale models of the buildings they design, making an Action Plan Collage™ allows you to visually articulate all the steps of a detailed project. Keep in mind, for the goal to come true, it is extremely important to take this next step of actualizing a detailed plan; including a start date and a target completion date. Having a clear visual understanding of all the steps and the time frame, will help you to pace your work flow appropriately, avoiding the stress caused by haphazard mistakes and the last-minute scrambles. Your plan should also identify what you need to learn and the people who will be your support team during the project.

Unlike the typical to-do list, creating an Action Plan Collage is a kind and supportive process. As you make your collage, breaking all the steps down with elements, you are also breaking down anxiety related to the work ahead. You create a clear, detailed plan, which the vagueness of a to-do list could never accomplish. This will significantly reduce anxieties throughout the project while instilling a sense of anticipation, causing you to look forward to the completed goal. You will tap directly into your creative intelligence to imagine all the tasks and how to accomplish them, allowing you to witness and emotionally accept how creative and brilliant you are. Your Action Plan Collage will be your beacon, visually illuminating the necessary steps and the final cumulative outcome. It will guide and support you throughout the project and be a continuous source of inspiration, motivation, and excitement along the way.

Laurie Kanyer, *House Fly*, 2017, Collage, Doug + Laurie Kanyer Art Collection

Idris Veitch, *Twin Flame (Pulling and Shoving)*, 2020, Collage, Doug + Laurie Kanyer Art Collection

Karen Coull, *Stitch In Time*, 2020, Collage Embroidery, Doug + Laurie Kanyer Art Collection

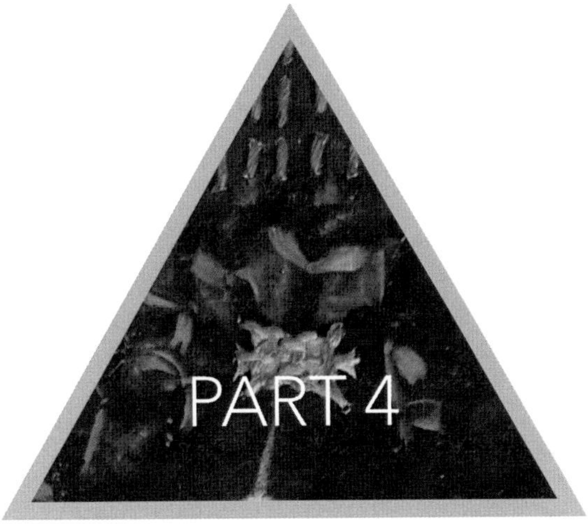

Reflections—Real Life Collage Testimonies

Two definitions of the word reflection are: the return of light or sound waves from a surface and a thought, idea, or opinion formed as a result of meditation.

The Reflections to follow are just that, light returned off of the surface of the precious souls who shared their stories of how collage transformed their emotions and life experiences. The Reflections were written after a period of meditation, where the authors pondered their hardships and joys, and then documented for you to read here how the use of collage healed and inspired.

You will find stories of deep pain and amazing surprises. You will find heartfelt testimony on how collage was not only therapeutic, but lifesaving—helping the authors survive and thrive in time of trials. The hope in offering you these Reflections is as you read them, your journey of exploring collage will be reinforced and upheld. You will find you are not the only one looking for answers to heavy questions. You will see how the use of collage is an answer.

MY ESCAPE

by Kellette Elliott, Collagist

I make collages because it is an escape, it is a therapy for me. It has helped me get through some really difficult times in my life. In the summer of 2018, my mom was diagnosed with stage 4 cancer. I had already been making collages daily, but now it became a connection between her and me, it gave us something to talk about each day. I started seeing that I was dealing with her diagnosis through my collage. I would make her collages that represented the mother-daughter relationship and she really appreciated those.

So when we knew her days were numbered, I noticed my collages were getting more emotional. I tended to use a lot of explosions; the world was exploding around me. I even remember making collages in the car on the way to the funeral home-that's how I was dealing with this terrible loss.

Since then I have had some medical issues as well, including chronic back pain. I make collages about 2 pm every day, I find it helps me forget about the pain for a couple of hours. I noticed I was making a lot of collages featuring a woman's back. I did not know why I was drawn to that subject until days later. My collages become narratives about my life whether I realize it or not. I don't see myself stopping making collages anytime soon because I depend on them.

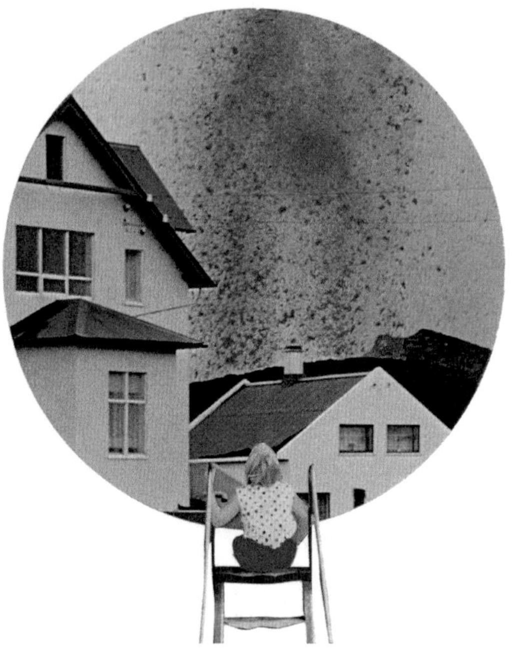

Kellette Elliott, *Explosive*, 2019

Kellette Elliott, *Vulnerability*, 2020

COLLAGING THROUGH A PANDEMIC

by Susan Lerner, Collagist

I always knew that collage was a cathartic and meditative medium. I could spend endless hours cutting photos from vintage magazines, accurately following lines of an image and meticulously slicing into books and maps. But it wasn't until the Covid-19 pandemic that I realized how much I needed to collage. Like most during 2020, my mind has been preoccupied with the pandemic, Black Lives Matter protests, the death of RBG [Ruth Bader Ginsberg] and everything leading up to the US Election. Sequestered away, my daily collage practice seemed mundane so I cut and cut and cut until I had piles of hundreds of images.

As life continued to implode, I decided to express my frustration, rage and helplessness through collage. By channeling my energy into creating images in the context of today's issues, I was able to process my feelings. My typical style includes the use of vintage imagery, so paired with the contentious matters of the day, the series Americana was born. The connection to past and present is always a theme in my work and it continues here with issues that have been lingering for decades. In addition, I limited the palette to red, white, blue and black and added ink, colored pencil and acrylic paint, enabling me to symbolically focus on the state of the union and its political ramifications.

This collage, *Hidden in Plain Sight*, was selected for the cover of a recently published zine titled *Americana*. The 'covid' virus is front and center, taking space in the sky of stars. The bottom left shows viruses that have started to usurp the sky and the country. The man fishing literally catches the virus as he sits upon a coffin-like box, draped in the stripes of the American Flag.

Susan Lerner, *Hidden in Plain Sight*, 2020, Collage, Doug + Laurie Kanyer Art Collection

ORIGIN STORY

by CP Harrison, Collagist

"It took me four years to paint like Raphael, but a lifetime to paint like a child." – Pablo Picasso

October 11, 2020 – For five months I had been working with author, artist and counselor Laurie Kanyer on this project, of which we are both very excited. Kanyer has written, what we were calling at the time, collage guided exercises for a book titled C*ollage Care: Transforming Emotions and Life Experiences Using Collage.*

I am in my studio some 2,000 miles away from where Kanyer is writing the book. I act as both lab tech and test subject working through the exercises. I exercise. (Are they clear / Do they matter / Are they doable?)

I start my day in the lab with a fresh exercise called Permission to Play. I am an artist, I keep a toe in immaturity, this will be cake.

The directive for guided exercise Permission to Play begins with the instructions to notice what happens when you use crayons or colored markers to scribble on a substrate for "five full minutes." Fun, easy, of course! It's a Sunday, I should play.

Five minutes is a surprisingly long time to scribble. I eye the clock.

My thoughts become audible –

"Maybe I shouldn't have used a Sharpie."
"Has it really only been 2 minutes?"
"That is a freakin' ton of red!"
"I'll have to re-do this one."
"5 minutes is probably too much!"
"How is this going to collage?"
"This is garbage, it looks like a crime scene!"
"This isn't art, this isn't anything!"
"This can't be right!"

Reaching the five-minute mark, something…happens.

[cue the clinking and crashing of Forrest Gump's braces]

There is no "right!" It hits me like a ton of red markers.

When did I, the page ripping, paste-slinging, décollage fanatic, begin to worry about what was "right" in collage? I asked myself, "where did I get these self-imposed rules and why?" "That's not why I walk into the studio," I said to myself. "I'm fun! Where's the fun?"

And I flash to being 4 years old at my Mimi's kitchen table.

We didn't have a lot of money to spend on toys while my mom was away at work but my grandmother had an artist's eye. To stand in for a new toy, my Mimi and I would cut out the characters on my cereal boxes. Before long I had quite the collection of Toucan Sam, Tony the Tiger and Boo Berries. I had an entire world of colored and collaged scenes for these sugary cereal stars to play in. I could make them anything. This is where I wanted to remember.

Back in the real world - 2020 was a mess. The psychic trauma was thick —constant and oppressive. And while these are certainly issues we will address in our art, we mustn't lose sight of play. If we lose sight of play the bastards win!

Play is freedom. Play is collage. Play is a childhood we recall or one of which we only dreamed. Play is the little kid dancing in line at the bank. Don't forget to give yourself permission. Besides, you'll never be in line with these people again.

CP Harrison, *Disintegration Anxiety*, 2020, Collage, Doug + Laurie Kanyer Art Collection

MOMENT OF REVELATION

by Kathy Starr, MFA, Collagist

Forty-one years ago, I was diagnosed with an autoimmune disorder of the adrenal glands called Addison's disease. My life has been full and rewarding but my condition is challenging and requires a close eye medically.

The year 2019 was a particularly difficult one for me. By the end of the summer, I was clinically depressed and struggling to face each day. It was during that time that Laurie invited me to her home to make a collage.

I sat at her dining room table, cutting out elements from the pages of the magazine that jumped out at me. I seemed to remember gravitating to the color black and pointed shapes. She reassured me that I didn't have to worry about how it turned out. I didn't know at the time that she was sitting with me but had no intentions herself of constructing a collage with a specific theme or subject. She was just being present with me as I found the story of my experience in the pages of the magazine. When I finished pasting the pieces on the paper, she asked me to explain to her what my collage meant. You could visually see how dark I had been feeling inside.

That day I went away with magazines, paper to build collages, glue and what felt like an infusion of HOPE. Focusing on the physical act of cutting, arranging and pasting the pieces was a welcomed distraction from focusing on how I was feeling.

Making collages quickly became part of my wellness care.

I was relieved to discover there was no "right or wrong way" to make the collage. I felt no pressure to make something that would appeal to or impress others. I was playing. It was judgment-free.

Making collages was like a treasure hunt for me, each collage always revealed something new to me. I wondered what would appear? Nothing was planned, no theme was required and I just followed the clues by paying attention to what jumped out at me.

Without even realizing it, I began to experience joy and hope and that was reflected in my images. I loved the colors, the shapes and the many ways that they could be arranged or rearranged. The collages were a revelation of my inner growing stability and the lifting of the depression.

Kathy Starr, *Dreams*, 2019, Collage, Doug + Laurie Art Collection

PIVOTING WITH SCISSORS

by Jennifer Sampson, MFA
Collagist, Author, CUT IT OUT: THEATRICAL SET COLLAGES

My hands wouldn't stop trembling. I was one year into a debilitating chronic illness, and I realized that my health would most likely not improve. So my hands trembled and my mind raced with this fresh grief. I started cutting and pasting collages which evoked feelings of isolation, loss, and pain. However, I noticed that while cutting and pasting I wasn't aware of my symptoms, my mind quieted, and my hands steadied. I even felt sparks of joy. Soon I was filling sketchbook after sketchbook with a variety of themed images.

I am now three years into my illness, and stepping into my art room is like holding Mary Poppins's hand and jumping into a chalk drawing. Colors brighten and stories come to life. I get to create little worlds on paper or in three dimensional Theatrical Set Collages. Then, when my symptoms overtake me, the rain washes the chalk away, and I must step away and rest.

The practice of collage reminded me of what I had forgotten: the importance of play, the absolutely essential act of seeking joy regardless of one's circumstances.

Jennifer Sampson, *We Keep Going Around in Circles*, 2020, Theatrical Set Collage, Doug + Laurie Kanyer Art Collection

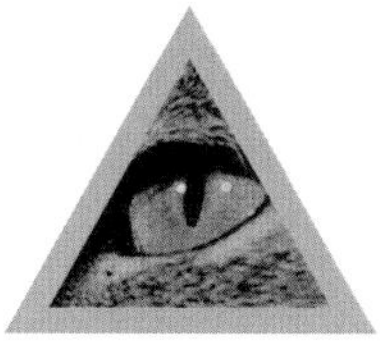

CAT'S-EYE VIEW

by Matt McCarthy, Collagist

I started making collage because it is a light in the darkness, and an escape from the norm. I was interested in how the act of combining disparate objects could create experiences outside of our own existence. Collage allows me to work in a surreal realm that feels both familiar and extraordinary.

I'm often asked why I use cats as the primary subject matter of my collage work. It began by observing my own cats and realizing that they're not so different from us humans. For millennia cats have protected us and our property from pests, yet that alone does not account for their universal admiration. There is an intangible quality to our fascination with cats. I believe, unlike other household pets, humans see themselves in the personalities of cats.

With this idea in my head, I adopted domestic felines as a surrogate in my work, using them to explore my own feelings through emotions shared between species. The cats in my pieces allow me to play with angry, petty, and selfish impulses in a way I would never act out in real life. By increasing their size, I attempt to amplify all of their traits, making them transparent in a way I don't feel comfortable being. Cats don't care about society or rules. They're unapologetically themselves. An unexpected benefit of making cat collages is that I've connected with people around the world over a shared love of felines. Cats are a global language that crosses all borders, a sacred subliminal spark that speaks to us all. Collage helped me escape reality, cats gave me my voice, and together they helped me find my people.

Matt McCarthy, *Uninvited Guest*, 2019, Collage, Doug + Laurie Kanyer Art Collection

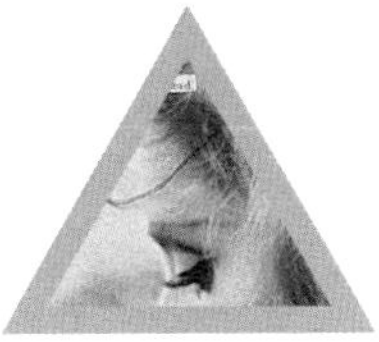

POST CONCUSSION COLLAGE THERAPY

by Juliette Pestel, Collagist

On December 16th, 2017, I was preparing for the opening of the Collage Garden in the Netherlands, when a wooden beam fell on my head, causing a concussion. I managed to do the opening speech, but soon noticed I was sensitive to light, sound and had a splitting headache. I took it easy for the next 2 weeks, lying on the couch with the cats, curtains drawn, lights very low. I stayed away from my phone and I couldn't read more than a few sentences. I was scared, but tried to stay positive. So I made a collage: *At The End Of Her Rope, Julie Noticed There Was Still A Little Balance Left.*

On January 4th, I was supposed to teach a collage workshop. It never happened because the evening before the workshop, I collapsed. The sensitivity to light, sound, and movement worsened. I was nauseous and couldn't focus on text for more than 1 sentence. I had memory issues as well and was really depressed, tired and extremely low on energy. I felt awful.

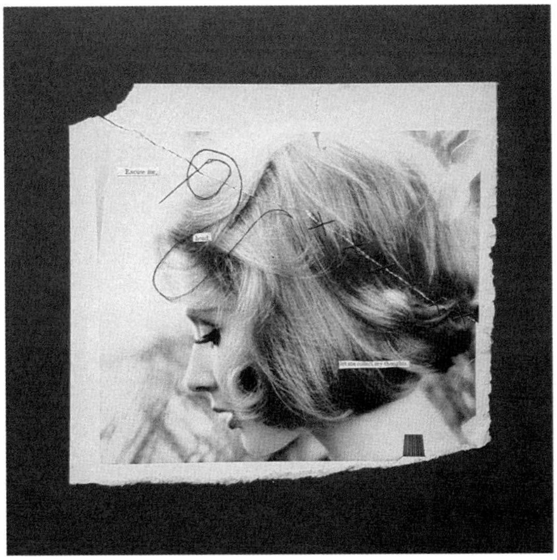

Juliette Pestel, *Absent While Mending*, 2017, Collage, Doug + Laurie Kanyer Art Collection

It took me almost 8 months to recover from most of the symptoms. I announced my absence from social media a month later with a simple collage I made, *Absent While Mending*. It took me more than a week to complete. It was so difficult to focus. After I had finished, I felt a spark of positivity and felt I had achieved something important. The collage helped me come back through the dark for a moment.

Making collages gave me purpose, lifted my spirits and I felt an important part of myself starting to heal while creating. With each collage, I felt I could focus a bit more. Two and half months after the concussion, I announced my partial comeback on social media with the collage *Post Concussion Behavior: Juliette Is Sort of Semi Half Back* in which I tried to capture how I felt at that point: sort of ok, but not totally recovered. Four months after the concussion, I started to teach collage workshops again, slowly but surely. It took me 8 months to feel I was almost as good as new. I only had some difficulties with focus and memory left. Making collages helped my recovery enormously.

Juliette Pestel, *At the End of Her Rope, Julie Discovered There was Still a Little Balance Left*, 2017, Collage, Doug + Laurie Kanyer Art Collection

I HEALED THROUGH THE POWER OF COLLAGE!

by Julia Payne, Artist

"I was really angry and hurt by someone the other day. I came down to my studio area and I just started cutting and gluing. When I was done, I felt like I had released all of that spew! And then I had a good laugh. There is the healing power of collage!" (See images to the right: the fist is the collage made when angry, the second a few days later.)

▼

"I have a friend who broke both her legs and spent her hospitalization and rehab working on a series of leg journals. Collage was perfect—paper, book and glue stick. Another who has been bed-ridden for almost two months and produced sometimes a dozen collages a day. In my own experience, I used collage to produce a series on ancestors, honoring those who were gone, but "I am here because they had been here!"

▼

"The collagist CP Harrison told me that he had been a poet until he had run out of ways to express himself with words. It was then that he turned to collage. I can so relate to that."

▼

"When I am feeling ravaged, I go down to the studio and I let the colors speak to me. Something arrives on the paper within minutes. I wait and something comes. I feel at peace, that is the power of collage."

▼

"In looking at my Instagram posts, they have become a journal of my feelings over the past 5 months, joy, sorrow, fear, anger, shock, hope."

▼

"I know collage as meditation, collage as healer, collage as truth-teller."

Julia Payne, *Angry! Hurt! Not Gonna Think!*, 2020, Collage

Julia Payne, *Meditation on Blues*, 2020, Collage

OUTSIDE OF SELF

by Kevin Sampsell, Author, Collagist

When I started collaging more in 2014, it was partly to find a new outlet of expression. I had just published a novel and was mostly known as a writer. But I needed a break from the exacting discipline of writing, like my brain yearned for some rest and a vacation. Making collages opened up a visual kind of playland for me. Working free and loose with combinations of images and other visual fragments, allowed me to see more and think less.

I found myself having fun again and I found myself looking at the world around me in a whole new way. Nature became more majestic, decay more interesting and emotions more abstract and malleable. I woke up each day thinking about different things I could collage with and I usually stayed up late, unaware of the hours slipping by, pleasantly looking at the piles of cut-up paper and imagining all the possibilities.

Over the years, my collage practice has got me through breakups, depression, death and creative slumps. I would say that the discovery of my love of collage is one of the five most important things to ever happen in my life—along with the birth of my son, discovering at 21 that I actually love to read, my work in the literary community and meeting my awesome tax lady when I was a financially-confused, thirty-something. Collage is something that I know will be part of the rest of my life. I even have a scissor tattoo on my right arm.

Kevin Sampsell, *Outside of Self*, 2020, Collage, Doug + Laurie Kanyer Art Collection

Kiki Buccini, *Blue for You*, 2019, Collage on Book Cover, Doug + Laurie Kanyer Art Collection

PART 5

Essays from Experts

"Life is like a collage. Its individual pieces are arranged to create harmony. Appreciate the artwork of your life."

—Amy Leigh Mercree

EXCERPT FROM CUTTING EDGES: CONTEMPORARY COLLAGE

by James Gallagher, Artist, Creative Director

Though it first gained popularity in the early 20th century, collage—defined as "an artistic composition made of various materials (such as paper, cloth or wood) glued on a surface" and derived from the French word for "to glue"—is a true reflection of the world we live in today. On our streets, in our stores and across our glowing computer and TV screens, images and information swirl around us at a faster pace than ever before—and the sheer magnitude of these images and information is relentless. Collage is all about the recycling, reinterpretation and reprocessing of our collective past, present and future. And, it is the medium for our time.

As we grow more accustomed to these three "re's," collage comes as a relief: a frozen moment that draws you in for a closer look. Collage is an unexpected yet strikingly appropriate means of channeling and processing the world around us. I discovered the medium by chance nearly 20 years ago, when I was working as an illustrator, with printmaking as my preferred medium. As a recent art school grad and new father inundated with deadlines, I had little time to get to the print shop (let alone anywhere else) so for one particular project, I began cutting apart old prints and piecing them together to form a new composition. The results completely reinvigorated my creativity, but it wasn't until nearly a decade later that the full extent of the medium's possibilities became apparent.

That year, as I was undergoing a period of personal struggle, one of the things that got me through those dark days was the act of cutting and pasting. There was something truly cathartic about stripping images down to their simplest forms and then building them back up again; collage was the perfect metaphor for what I was also doing with my life, day in and day out.

This combination of knife, paper and glue, coupled with an urge for expression, yielded exciting results. Collage became a way of channeling and processing the beauty, ugliness, solitude and desire that I saw swirling past me in my life in New York. My constructed scenes often focused on personal space, physical relationships and enigmatic situations. I investigated—and continue to investigate—human form, personal identity and private dramas. This is where my story lines live and the scenes are layered from shreds of real life. It was the perfect representation of me on a page: both raw and refined.

Prologue 2021

Another decade has passed and the medium of collage has continued to grow in ways I could not have imagined. Its popularity in our current digital landscape has paved the way for untold virtual gatherings and online collectives and helped connect like-minded image-makers from all corners of the globe. Being a part of this collage community has been truly rewarding and I'm honored to have artists reach out to me seeking advice...from university students working on thesis projects, to established artists who are just discovering collage as a new form of expression. I'm thankful that my experience can help others find their voice and feel fortunate that this art form continues to inspire, challenge and inform me as an artist and as a human.

James Gallagher, *Aunt Julie*, 2019, Collage, Doug + Laurie Kanyer Art Collection

COLLAGE, MUCH LIKE HUMANITY

by Wyatt Kanyer, MSW, LSWAIC, TCTSY-F

Collage, much like humanity, is comprised of endless paths and possibilities. It makes sense then, to offer collage as an exploratory medium, both artistically and therapeutically. Perhaps collage can even serve as a space where people who have survived hardship can express this survivorship without the limitations, definitions and expectations of verbal processing.

In his book *On Becoming a Person: A Therapist's View of Psychotherapy*, Carl Rogers writes that, "a person is a fluid process, not a fixed and static entity; a flowing river of change, not a block of solid material; a continually changing constellation of potentialities, not a fixed quantity of traits" (Rogers, 1961). When a survivor (we've all survived something) opens a book like *Collage Care*, perhaps they have faced a series of limiting expectations. Perhaps they have navigated therapeutic modalities that did not honor their needs or acknowledge their progress. Collage, a medium that values and uplifts choice-making, is a trauma-sensitive form of artistic expression. In addition to choice-making, collage offers opportunities to engage most of a person's near senses (seeing the piece of paper; touching the scissors and cut-outs; hearing the sounds of scissors cutting paper/material and pages turning; noticing the scents of the books, magazines, publications and glue/adhesive). This choice-based sensory experience also offers an opportunity to re-story or revalue one's biologically engineered signals and responses.

Also, when considering Rogers' interpretation of personhood, one may recognize that a "fixed" object (let's say a photo in a magazine) can magically become "fluid" using collage (by reshaping the photo into a shape the creator chooses). For me as a clinical social worker who has the honor of working with people who have survived trauma, collage is a miracle, as it has the potential to restore choice-making and power to people who have navigated a life in which choice-making and power were unexpectedly removed. Collage also offers an opportunity to instill hope and foster what Deb Dana calls "the rhythm of regulation" (Dana, 2018), our autonomic nervous system's biologically engineered ability to create safe/brave attachment to our environment. This rhythm of regulation (also called our ventral vagal response, or the "social engagement system") tends to activate with the help of non-verbal sensory experiences—soothing and predictable sounds/vocal tones or scents, choice-based touch, neutral environmental cues and images. Maybe you're recognizing the parallels between collaging and this social engagement activation.

Collage Care's author also happens to be my mom, so the 100-plus tools here extend beyond my training and practice and into my personal experience. In fact, although I am not a collage artist, I recognize that collage has imprinted on my own social engagement system, as it represents the gift of secure attachment in my life. When I was about 10 years old, my mom offered me an opportunity to set up materials for parenting classes she facilitated. Among those materials were magazines, scissors, tape and glue. At that time, I assumed the group was reading the magazines for entertainment during breaks or something along those lines. Little did I know that my mom was collaging with the women she worked with, most of them trauma survivors themselves, offering them a chance to express non-verbally. I even learned recently that she collaged with high school students when she taught human development in the 1980s.

So, whether you find yourself on these pages of *Collage Care* as a collage artist, a clinician, a collage enthusiast, a survivor or anyone in between, perhaps you will recognize an opportunity to choose from the endless shapes you might take on this journey of self-awareness through collage.

Wyatt Kanyer, *With Love*, 2017, Collage, Doug + Laurie Kanyer Art Collection

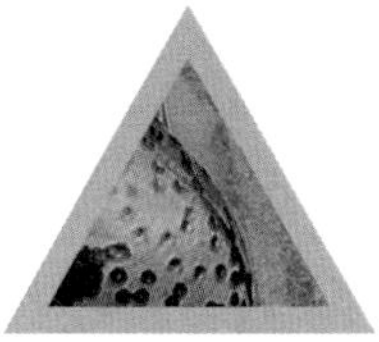

IT'S ALL COLLAGE

by Katie Blake, MS, MLIS

Artist and professor Todd Bartel says, "Ever since the Big Bang, it's all collage!"[1] For this writing, we are going to fast forward to the emergence of people and state unequivocally that all collage is about making connections; and that concept explains the continued existence of humans. Connections as a means of recognition, recognition to build up safety, safety to survive, and surviving long enough to evolve. It really is all collage.

Accepting that it is our nature to collage,[2] what then is art collage? As Penelope Wickson cautions this medium is "a form of art that is exceptionally hard to define due to its vast scope, complex relationship with academic tradition and ability to evade any confinement through terminology due to the very nature of its production. Indeed, the creation of collage extends far beyond its etymology."[3] If we agree that it "evades any confinement through terminology" and that it is inherently human to collage, let it be acceptable that art theories (which want so much to put things into perspective to fence off movements and schools) should praise that collage as an art form is a challenge. The practice and materials used typically reflect the time and trend and come from a place of need or desire of the individual. When writing about collage works created between 1500 and 1900, (*Collage Before Modernism*) Freya Gowrley includes in her discussion all manner of media and manifestations such as scrapbooks and decoupaged wood screens. Instead of falling into habitual art history canon fodder of which works surpassed craft and could be considered 'fine art,' she makes a point of stating that, "such objects were a crucial means by which people expressed their emotions, both for themselves and those with whom they were intimate. Collage could therefore be a highly personal form of artistic practice."[4] More contemporarily, consider the practice of collage by the artist Daniel Fountain, who not only looked at antecedents to find connections in the how and why of art making, but also considered how audiences might perceive the way in which he treated the media he used. He states of his collage work, *Eve and Adam* (2015) that his process could, "be seen as one of aggression (to rip, to tear) – [however] I find the act of reconfiguring (to stitch, to glue) both reparative and therapeutic."[5] What better way is there to understand and learn about a 'fine art' than those works which are made significant by connections to us and our intimates.

Instead of holding back on the practice of making collage because of perceptions of what is art or is not, let this medium and this book be an invitation to start making connections.

[1] BostonVoyager. 2018. Art & Life with Todd Bartel. 7Dec2018. http://bostonvoyager.com/interview/art-life-todd-bartel/
[2] 'Collage' by its contemporary definitions infers glue as a binder; but we recognize and value collage as a medium, as a concept `1 and are avid seekers of it in all manifestations.
[3] Wickson, Penelope. 2019. Exhibition Review: I'll just get them a Big Bag of Scraps: Cut and Paste: 400 Years of Collage, Scottish National Galleries of Modern Art, Edinburgh.
Available at: https://collageresearchnetwork.wordpress.com/blog/
[4] Gowrley, Freya. Collage Before Modernism. Cut and Paste: 400 Years of Collage. 2019. Pg 29.
[5] Fountain, Daniel. The Art of Hannah Höch: Queering Collage via Jack Halberstam. June 13, 2019.
Available at: https://collageresearchnetwork.wordpress.com/blog/

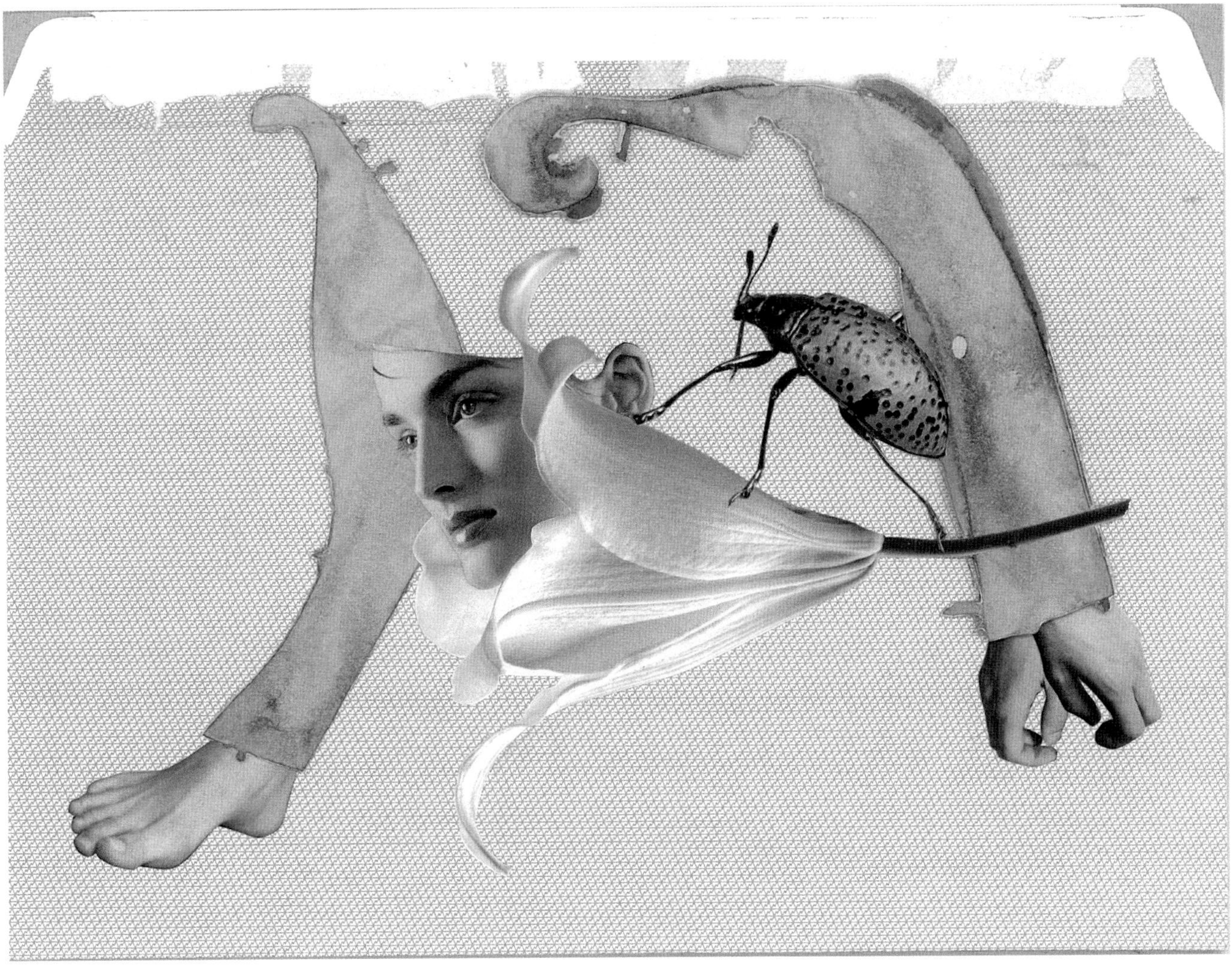

Katie Blake, *Untitled*, 2015, Collage, Doug + Laurie Kanyer Art Collection

COLLAGE IS TRANSFORMATION

by Todd Bartel, MFA

Collage Care brings together the disparate fields of psychology (self-care), art (collage) and the history of both. This book signals an invocation, an affirmation and an invitation. It joins cutting edge art-historical precedents with evidence-based therapy practices as a new platform to explore and reflect.

Affirmation? The fields of art and psychology have made advances in the last century and these respective fields have often co-mingled and enhanced each other. Empirically speaking, in 1998, I penciled my first drafts of glue taxonomy inspired by nearly a century of fine art collage evolution in an attempt to find correlative connections to neuroscientist Paul D. MacLean's Triune Brain Theory:

- Reptilian Complex (Basal Ganglia): pattern-based glue
- Paleomammalian Complex (Limbic System): emotional glue, memorial glue
- Neomammalian Complex (Neocortex): alpha-numeric glue, visual glue, associative glue, conceptual glue, philosophical glue, moral glue

Revisiting art history through such lenses yielded new ideas and understanding.

I met Laurie Kanyer about a year after lecturing at Kolaj Fest 2018—a symposium about collage. We quickly found mutual interest—belief in the power of collage to transform. After learning about Kanyer's research and use of collage as a vehicle for emotional transformation and problem-solving, I prompted her to write this book.

As early as 1986, Laurie Kanyer brought the canon of collage into the realm of psychology in her educational and counseling practice. Throughout the course of her career, Kanyer has identified over 125 ways of using collage as a vehicle for self-reflection, healing and transformation.

This book calls on art history to redress the attitudes that look down upon collage for its "easiness," its perceived "lack of originality," its "dependence upon found materials" and its supposed "lack of seriousness." Such misunderstandings and surface assumptions misappropriate the power of connection, juxtaposition and transformation in collage. Collage is the most equitable form of communication ever developed because it can incorporate anything and it teaches the importance of seeing. With such widespread application of collage in contemporary art-making today and with such profound possibility for personal reflection, this book affirms the need for further identification, application and appreciation.

Invocation? *Collage Care* is a germ seed for future work between these separate fields of study. Now that this book has entered into physical existence, it invokes discourse and cross-pollination, having implications for understanding each canon in a new light.

Invitation? Anyone drawn to collage and these respective fields, anyone pulled to explore themself through a creative process and anyone wanting to engage in scholarship regarding the dovetailing of multi-curricular disciplines will find this material essential.

Collage Care celebrates the intersection of reflectivity, self-expressivity, communication, connectivity and the elastic possibility of combination. *Collage Care* welcomes the agglutination of anything experienced in life with readily available materials—things made by hand, mass-produced or found in nature—be they analog or virtual. When ideas, memories, emotions or associations become forces that guide the selection of and interaction between physical materials, the resultant collage is always a personal epiphany.

Todd Bartel, *Proclamation (Odd Fellows.29)*, 1983, Collage, Doug + Laurie Kanyer Art Collection

Ben DiNino, *Becoming One With Your Environment*, 2021, Collage, Doug + Laurie Kanyer Art Collection

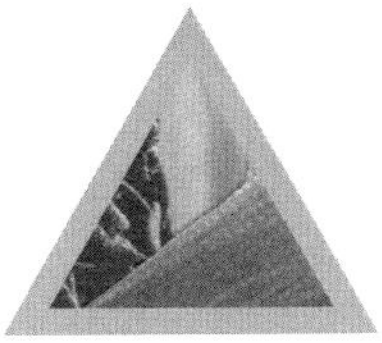

EPILOGUE

As long as there has been paper, people have been using it to document the most important aspects and milestone moments of their lives. Paper is important. For 400 years, people have been using paper to make collage as well. This is made evident by The National Galleries in Scotland with the first retrospective exhibition of collage in Europe. During the Victorian era, there were scrapbooks made by women as well as large screens designed at family gatherings (Growley, 2019). In the early 1900s, collage was used to communicate revolts against the abuses of governments, such as the Nazis (Quinn, 2019). By the mid century, collage took on the allure of surrealism with the fascination of expressing dreams. Presently, we find ourselves in a period in which using collage has become a serious tool for exploring one's life and emotions (Babla, 2020).

Having read this book, you now have insight as to how using paper, pieced together in a collage, will assist in transforming your emotions and life events. What you have read in *Collage Care* here is what I observed in my clinical observations and how I used college with my clients. This is just the beginning in understanding the deep and enduring value of collage. You will discover additional ways collage helps to transform emotions and life experiences. Please let me know what you discover so we can build together on this research. I know from my professional and personal experiences, that embracing collage will establish new and different ways to better communicate with others and understand oneself. I witnessed how collage changed lives, time and time again, in my practice. It will change your life too.

"Given the vagaries of memory, life itself is a collage.
Perhaps that is part of the reason why putting
disparate images together and makin
something new of them can be
so involving, meaningful
and therapeutic."

—Dr. Rachel Morris

ACKNOWLEDGEMENTS

It is with great honor and respect that I acknowledge the help and support of the following individuals.

The insight and wisdom of Todd Bartel and Andrea Burgay ignited the inspiration for this book.

My husband Doug Kanyer, who is a remarkable human, funded these efforts and patiently listened through the joys of book writing and the hardships. His generosity made this book possible.

Wyatt Kanyer, my son, who became a social worker and has his own massive caseload, is now doing the work I used to do with the benefit of the research and insight we now have in 2020. He brought encouragement from a professional perspective and immediately saw the truth of what this book is about.

To Kathy Starr, thank you for the hours of discussing this material and all your encouragement. I went to Kathy any time I experienced a snag. She, having used collage in her life to support her emotional well-being, helped me to clarify my thoughts.

After getting a good start on the content, I began to share this project on Instagram. Collagist CP Harrison reached out to offer help. I recognized I needed a creative person with a background in counseling to test the material. CP tested the Gems in this book and made collages using the guided exercises for the forthcoming workbooks. CP has spent countless hours in his studio examining the truths you read within these pages.

Jennifer Waldsmith is the designer who first worked with me early in the process to establish a look for the book before the content was even completed; making it tangible and real with her designs.

John Baule, the initial editor, offered structure and clarity to the material. Having worked with John since 2007 on numerous projects, we have a partnership that is rare and beautiful.

It is with deep admiration that I acknowledge the work of Sarah Best as the co-creator of this book. Sarah is a collagist that wrote her capstone paper regarding particular neural systems in the brain and the emotional benefits of the use of collage. She understood from her studies what this book is about. Sarah is not only a gifted writer but also a gifted editor. She took my observations and helped to bring you the material in this book.

Lillian Cassidy has been in my life since 1996 and has been a friend and colleague. She has proofread many thousands of my words. Her process of proofreading is to read each word aloud, every word! To me this means the words of insight in this book have been spoken into the collective air we breathe—our very life force!

Neuroscientist, Dr. Matthew Caudill of Baylor College of Medicine in Houston, TX, USA verified my research on what parts of the brain benefit from the use of collage.

I am truly grateful to the people who read this book, assisted with proofreading, and helped to check citations. Their knowledge of the subject provided needed discernment that shaped the integrity of this volume. To Jen Gouge, Katie Blake, Celia Crane, Kathy Starr, Kacylia Pistoia, Dennis Busch, Teri Henderson, Jennifer Sampson, Greg Traw, Dr. Freya Gowrley, Teri Henderson, Sheila Darcy, Matt McCarthy, Dana Caldera, Dawn Kugler, Tanja Ulbrich, Hollie Chastain, Emily Shoemaker, Erin Houghtaling, Jasmine Romero, Connie Dawson, Clive Knights, Claire Standish, Mimi Shapiro, Miranda Millward, Monique Vettraino, Fred Free, Kelly Schaub and Steven Rudin, thank you for your insight and support.

Shane Hicks, a professional consultant to a number of my most recent projects, helped tremendously with the photo production for this book. Many of the collages for this book were masterfully prepared by Shane.

I also thank Jeannie Liu for her time in consultation and encouragement. It was your insight that ignited the beginning of the writing in April 2020.

I thank the publishers of *Kolaj Magazine* for featuring articles on this subject matter in Issues 18 and 24.

Thank you to JuSt Design, Senior Designers of this book. Your professionalism, enthusiasm, and attention to detail helped to support this book. Our work together allowed for our best selves to do some very important work together. I am deeply grateful for all your hard work and look forward to many books to follow.

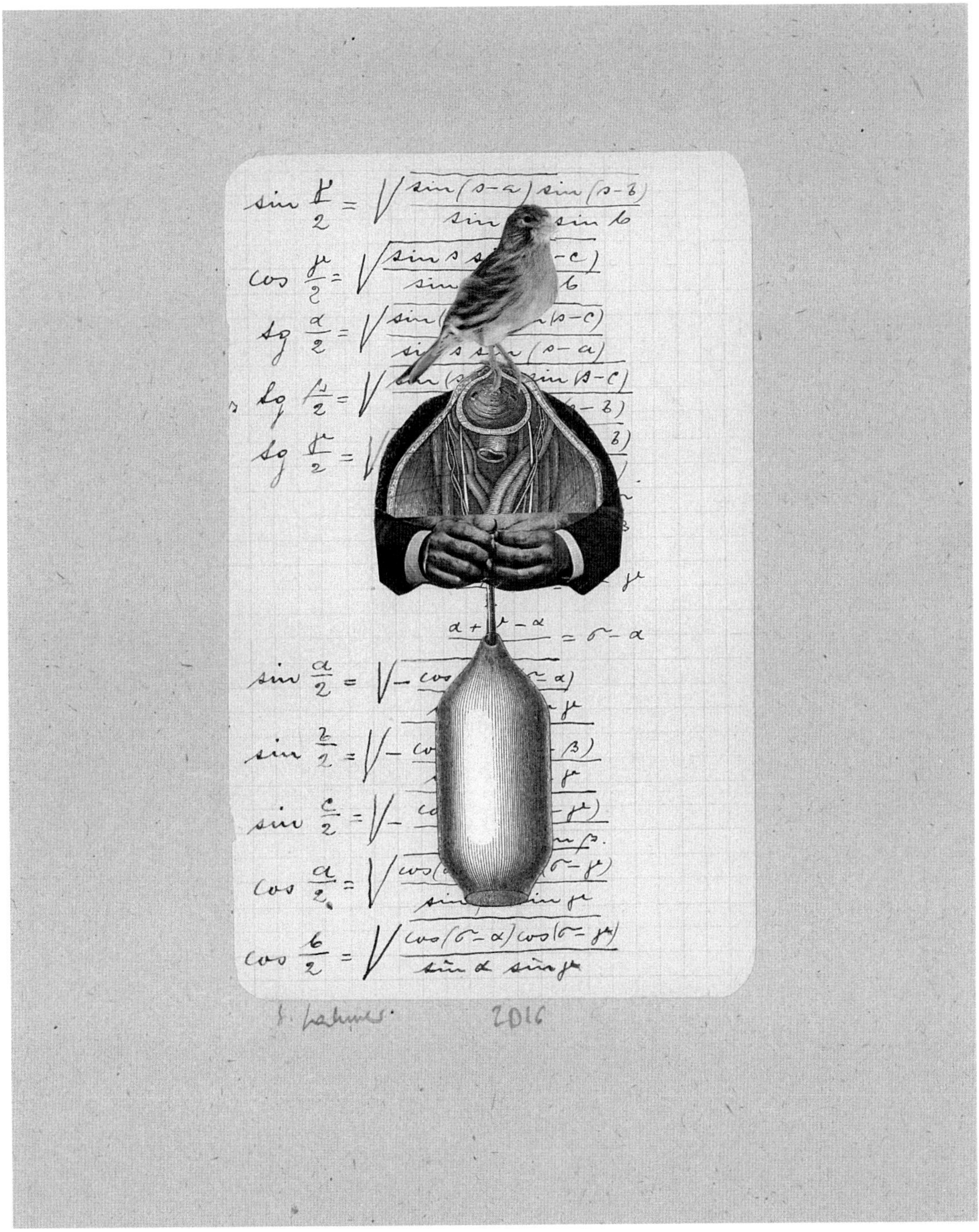

Susanna Lakner, *Bird*, 2016, Collage, Doug + Laurie Kanyer Art Collection

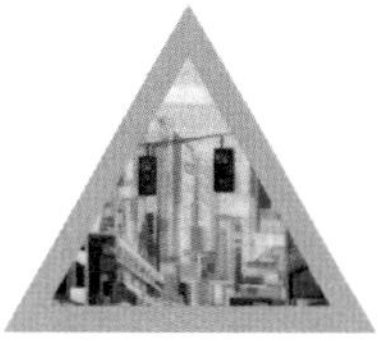

RESOURCES

COLLAGE TECHNIQUE BOOKS

Chastain, Hollie, *If You Can Cut, You Can Collage: From Paper Scraps to Works of Art*, Quarry Books, 2017

Moore, Alannah, *The Collage Ideas Book*, Ilex Press, 2018

Speight, Bev, *Project Collage: 50 Projects to Spark Your Creativity*, Ilex Press, 2019

COLLAGE EXCHANGE BOOK

Zach Collins (Author, Designer), Laura Tringali Holmes (Editor), *We Said Hello and Shook Hands*, Self Published, 2015. This book gives a beautiful example of collaboration and community building that takes place in collage exchanges.

WORKSHOPS - ONLINE LECTURES ON COLLAGE AND EMOTIONS

Collage artist and retired psychiatrist Steven Rudin explores collage as a metaphor for memory and identity. Rudin leads workshops titled The Psychology of Collage, both online and in the classroom. Seeing collage as a motivator and teacher, Rudin encourages participants to envision their inner lives as an array of parts that can be put together in many ways.
Website: www.stevenrudin.com

MAGAZINES

Cut Me Up Magazine is a participatory magazine of visual call and response.
Website: www.cutmeupmagazine.com
Instagram: @cutmeupmagazine

Kolaj Magazine is a quarterly, printed, art magazine reviewing and surveying contemporary collage with an international perspective.
Website: www.kolajmagazine.com
Instagram: @kolajmagazine

Plastikcomb Magazine is a biannual print magazine that features collage.
Website: www.plastikcombmag.com

Photo Trouvée Magazine is a publication that highlights the use of found photos as elements and the substrate for collage. The mission aims to showcase artists from around the world who work with found images and collecting stories of vintage ephemera. The magazine is distributed digitally. When purchased a PDF will be sent via email. It can be downloaded and kept forever to be read it electrically, or printed.
Website: www.phototrouveemagazine.com
Instagram: @phototrouveemagazine

ONLINE CLASSES AND RESOURCES

Black Collagists Arts Incubator was founded and is directed by Teri Henderson. The mission of the incubator is to highlight the work of Black artists making collage globally. The Black Collagists Arts Incubator serves as a platform for elevating Black collagists through regular features on Instagram (@blackcollagists), frequent features with Max-O-Matic on The Weird Show, curating exhibitions, and a forthcoming book. It is underwritten with a grant from Doug + Laurie Kanyer Art Collection.
Instagram: @blackcollagists

Collage artist Kelly Schaub founded collage-lab.com as a resource for collage artists around the world to learn about collage techniques. Collage-Lab offers online classes for all levels. Frequently sponsored are recurring Collage Scrap Exchange and Online Exhibit, a virtual collage materials scavenger hunt, monthly online collage Play Dates, free challenges, and international calls for collage artists. Additionally, it offers a yearlong online course about various collage techniques and a supportive Facebook Group for collagists.
Instagram: @mycollagelab

COLLAGE COLLECTIVES

Paris Collage Collective is an international collage community. Through collaborations and weekly creative projects, Paris Collage Collective wants to encourage creative expression and help build meaningful connections between like minded people.
Website: www.pariscollagecollective.com
Instagram: @pariscollagecollective

Edinburgh Collage Collective (EEC) is faciliated by collagist Rhed Fawell. ECC's aim is to develop an environment where like-minded collagists can share ideas and build creative opportunities. Through regular showcasing of artists' work and Open Call Projects, EEC hopes to excite and inspire interest in collage and open up a dialogue around the medium. EEC also encourages followers to reach out to one another and to connect independently, hopefully forging ties which can lead to future projects.
Website: www.edinburghcollagecollective.com
Instagram: @edinburghcollagecollective

COLLAGE COMMUNITIES PRINT RESOURCES

International Directory of Collage Communities (book) is a survey of collage networks, guilds, communities, and projects as well as online efforts and groups focused on collage research.
Directory: www.kolajmagazine.com/collage-communities
Directory print: shop.kasinihouseartshop.com/product/the-international-directory-of-collage-communities

ONLINE JOURNALS

Toombes.com is an online art journal curated by Niko Vartiainen, the Finnish collage artist and designer. Since the first post in 2016, the journal has showcased contemporary visual culture and its creators with a strong focus on collage and mixed media art.
Instagram: @toombescom

The Weird Show is an art platform dedicated to the showcase and exploration of contemporary collage through exhibitions, online and offline publishing, and workshops and sessions. In the process of mapping contemporary collage as a medium, we are especially interested in the blurred areas where collage touches other disciplines.
Website: www.theweirdshow.info
Instagram: @theweirdshowoffical

RESEARCH ON COLLAGE

The Collage Research Network is a network dedicated to supporting research being undertaken on collage made across the globe and at any time throughout its long history. The Network has a monthly newsletter, 381 hosts a blog, and runs a series of events.
Website: www.collageresearchnetwork.wordpress.com
Twitter: @Collage_Res_Net

COLLAGE SOCIETIES

The goal of the National Collage Society is to foster the appreciation and interest in the recognized medium of collage.
Website: www.nationalcollage.com

FINE ART COLLECTIONS FOCUSING EXCLUSIVELY ON COLLAGE

Doug + Laurie Kanyer Art Collection is one of very few private art collections focusing on collage exclusively.
Website: www.kanyerartcollection.com
Instagram: @kanyerartcollection

National Collage Society has a permanent teaching collection of collage housed at Kent State University in Kent, Ohio, USA.
Website: www.nationalcollage.com

INSTAGRAM

The founder of The Weird Show, Max-o-matic recommends Instagram as a lovely tool to discover more collage. #contemporarycollage or #collageart.

INSTITUTE

Kolaj Institute: The mission of Kolaj Institute is to support artists, curators, and writers who seek to study, document, and disseminate ideas that deepen our understanding of collage as a medium, a genre, a community, and a 21st century movement. We operate a number of initiatives meant to bring together the community, investigate critical issues, and raise collage' standing in the art world.
Website: www.kolajinstitute.org

VOCABULARY OF FEELING WORDS

abandoned
abhor
abused
accepted
adored
affectionate
affronted
afraid
aggravated
aghast
agitated
alarmed
alienated
alone
amazed
amused
angry
anguish
annoyed
anxious
appreciated
apprehensive
ardent
ashamed
aspire
astonished
at ease
awful
awkward
baffled
battered
beat
befuddled
belittled
belligerent
below par
bemused
bewildered
bitter
blamed
blissful
blue
bored
bothered
bottled up
branded
broken
bushed
calm
capable
cared for
cast off
cheapened
cheerful
cheerless
cheery
comforted
compassionate
competent
concerned
confident
conflicted
confused
constrained
contented
covetous
craving
critical
criticized
cross
crushed
cunning
cynical
debased
defeated
deficient
deflated
dejected
delirious
demoralized
depreciated
depressed
deserted
desolate
despair
desperate
despised
despondent
disappointed
disbelieving
disconcerted
discontent
discouraged
discredited
disenchanted
disgraced
disheartened
disinterested
disliked
dismal
disparate
dispassionate
displeased
disregarded
dissatisfied
distressed
distrustful
disturbed
done for
doubtful
doubting
down
downcast
downhearted
downtrodden
dread
dreadful
drowsy
ecstatic
edgy
elevated
embarrassed
empty
enraged
enthusiastic
envious
euphoric
excited
excluded
exhausted
exhilarated
exposed
exultant
fantastic
fearful
fervent
fine
fit
fond of
foolish
forlorn
forsaken
frantic
friendless
friendly
frightened
frustrated
fuming
furious
futile
glad
gloomy
glorious
good
grand
grateful
gratified
great
grieved
guilty
happy
hated
hatred
heartbroken
helpful
helpless
hesitant
hindered
hopeless
horrible
humble
humiliated
hurt
hypocritical
ignored
ill at ease
impaired
impatient
impotent
imprisoned
in the dumps
inadequate
incapable
incensed
incompetent
ineffective
inept
inferior
inflamed
infuriated
insecure
insignificant
intimidated
irritated
jazzed
jealous
jilted
jittery
jovial
joyful
jumpy
laughed at
left out
liable
liked
loathe
lonely
lonesome
longing
lost
lousy
loved
loving
low
mad
maligned
miffed
miserable
misunderstood
moved
mystified
needed
negative
neglected
nervous
numb
obsessive
obsolete
offended
on cloud nine
on edge
oppressed
optimistic
ostracized
outraged
overlooked
overwhelmed
panicky
passionate
perplexed
pleased
powerless
pressured
proud
put down
puzzled
reborn
rebuked
regret
rejected
rejuvenated
relaxed
relieved
repulsed
resented
resentful
restless
revengeful
ridiculed
ridiculous
rotten
run down
sad
saddened
satisfied
scared
self-conscious
selfish
sensual
serene
shaky
shocked
sickened
silly
skeptical
slandered
sleepy
slighted
snubbed
spiteful
startled
stifled
surprised
suspicious
swamped
tearful
tense
terrified
threatened
thrilled
tired
tormented
transcendent
triumphant
troubled
trusting
uncertain
uncomfortable
uncooperative
underrated
understood
uneasy
unhappy
unimportant
unloved
unnoticed
unqualified
unsatisfied
unsure
upset
uptight
want
wanted
warmhearted
warped
wary
whipped
worn-out
worried
worshipped
worthless
worthy
wounded
zoned

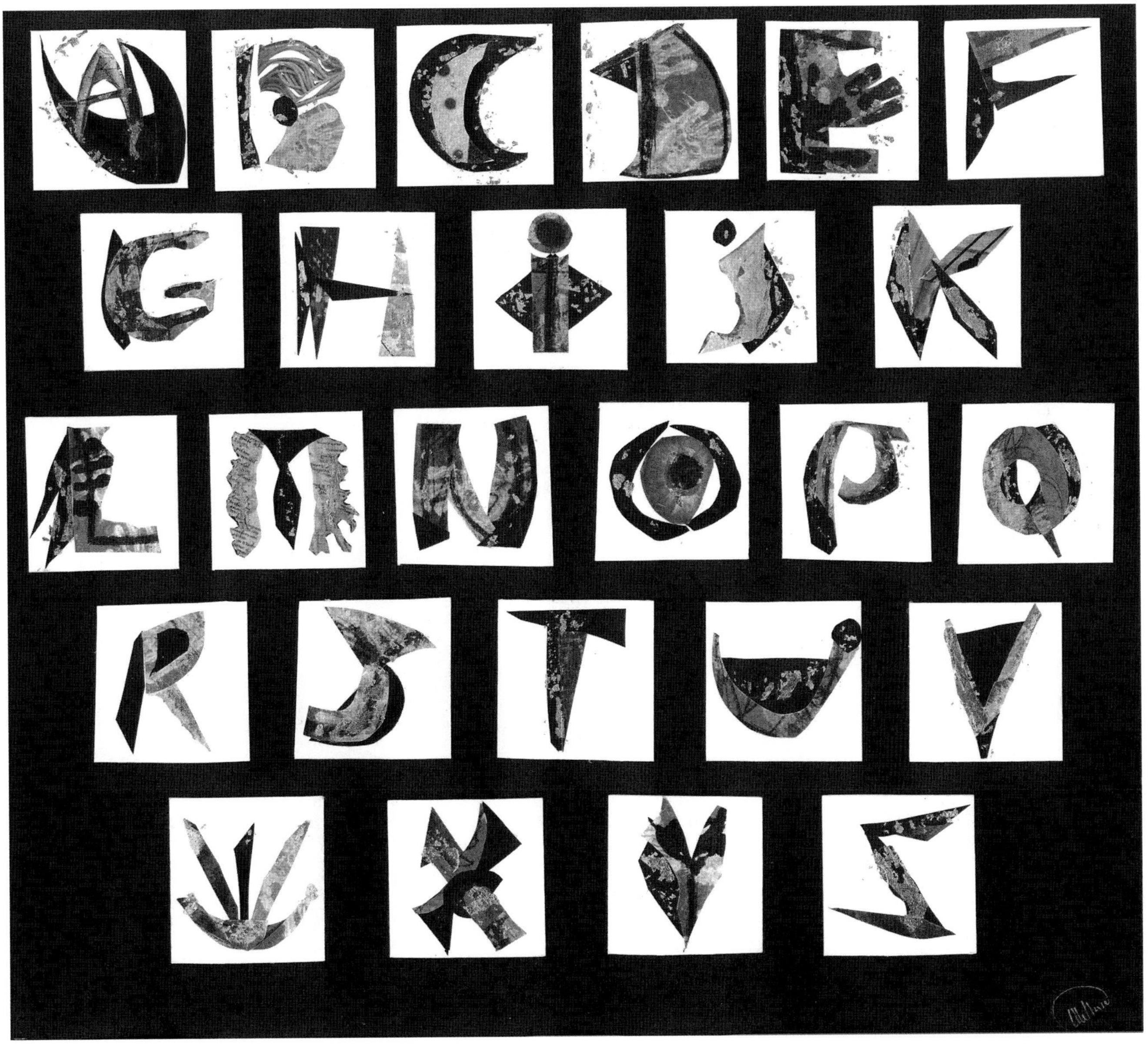

Isabelle Milkoff, *Alphabet for abécédaire*, 2020, Collage, Doug + Laurie Kanyer Art Collection

NOTES

Armor, R. (September 28, 1981). Some books are to be chewed and digested. Christian Science Monitor, https://www.csmonitor.com/1981/0928/092804.html.

Babla, A. (2009, May 29). Putting the pieces together: Collage as a mode in the treatment of trauma.*Collage Research Network.* https://collageresearchnetwork.wordpress.com/blog/.

Bertalanffy, L. (1968). *General systems theory: Foundations, development, applications.* Penguin.

Brackett, M. (2019). *Permission to feel: Unlocking the power of emotions to help our kids, ourselves, and our society thrive.* Celadon Books.

Brown, B. (2019, May 8). Shame thrives on secrecy, silence, and judgment. Shame can't survive being spoken. (Tweet) Twitter. https://twitter.com/BreneBrown/status/1126301981751029760.

Brown, B. (2020, 4 April). *Dr. Vivek Murthy on Loneliness and Connection.* [Interview] Unlocking Us. https://brenebrown.com/podcast/dr-vivek-murthy-and-brene-on-loneliness-and-connection/.

Burns, D. (1980). *Feeling good: The new mood therapy.* Harper.

Cherry, K. (2020, April 10). Left brain vs. right brain dominance. *Verywell Mind.* https://www.verywellmind.com/left-brain-vs-right-brain-2795005.

Cloninger C.R., Svrakic D.M. (2008). Personality disorders. *The Medical Basis of Psychiatry.* Humana Press.

Collage Research Network. (2018). *Meet our conveyors.* Collage Research Network. https://collageresearchnetwork.wordpress.com/meet-our-convenors/.

Dawson, C. (2016). Living beyond shame: rewriting rules. Balboa Press.

Dawson, C. (1994, May), Growing up again, parenting ourselves, parenting our children. Training, Passport to Parenting Memorial Hospital, Yakima WA.

Dymond, J. (2020, April 5). Coronavirus: Queen tells UK 'we will succeed' in fight, https://www.bbc.com/news/uk-52176222.

Eissinger, S. (2019, May 18). What is a STERB and why should you care? *Sagebrush Coaching.* http://www.sagebrushcoaching.com/what-is-a-sterb-and-why-should-you-care/.

Ferentz, L. (2014). *Letting go of self-destructive behaviors: A workbook of hope and healing.* Routledge.

Friedman, R. (2009). The grief recovery handbook: the action program for moving beyond death, divorce, and other losses including health, career, and faith. Collins Living.

Gowrley, Freya. (2019). Collage before modernism. Cut and paste: 400 years of collage, National Gallery of Scotland.

Graham, L. (n.d). The triangle of victim, recuser, persecutor—what it is and how to get out, Linda Graham, MFT, https://lindagraham-mft.net/triangle-victim-rescuer-persecutor-get/.

Hopper, R. (2018, July 18). We've started to uncover the true purpose of dreams. *New Scientist.* https://www.newscientist.com/article/mg23931873-300-weve-started-to-uncover-the-true-purpose-of-dreams/.

Hudson, R. & Riso D. R. (1999). *The wisdom of the enneagram: The complete guide to psychological and spiritual growth of the nine personality types.* Bantam.

Johnston, K. (1984). Hemingway and Freud: The tip of the iceberg. *The Journal of NarrativeTheory*, 14(1), 68-73.

Jones, D. (2020). The difference between triangles and triangulation: Family systems theory for church leaders, The Presbyterian Outlook, https://pres-outlook.org/2020/02/the-difference-between-triangles-and-triangulation-family-systems-theory-for-church-leaders/.

Kaczkurkin, A. N. (2015). Cognitive-behavioral therapy for anxiety disorders: An update on theempirical evidence. *Dialogues in Clinical Neuroscience*, 3(1), 337-343.

Kanyer, L. (2004). *Twenty-five things to do when grandpa passes away, mom and dad get divorced or the dog dies.* Chicago Review Press.

Kanyer, L. (2018). Collage saves. *Kolaj Magazine.* https://kolajmagazine.com/content/content/articles/collage-saves/.

Kasini-Kadour. R. (2019). Build a story, piece by piece, Doug + Laurie Kanyer Art Collection, Kolaj Magazine #27.

Kessler, D. (2019). *Finding meaning: The sixth stage of grief.* Scribner.

Knights, C. (2020), Personal conversation.

Krysa, D., & D'Aquino, A. (2014). Collage: contemporary artists hunt and gather, cut and paste, mash up and transform. Chronicle Books.

Kübler-Ross, E. (1969). *On death and dying, What the dying have to teach doctors, nurses, clergy & their own families.* Scribner.

Lowenstein, J. Purvis, C. & Rose, K. (2016). A systematic review on the relationship between antisocial, borderline and narcissistic personality disorder diagnostic traits and risk of violence to others in a clinical and forensic sample. *Borderline Personality Disorders and Emotion Dysregulation*, 3(14).

Mayo Clinic Staff. (2019). Stress relief from laughter? It's no joke. *Mayo Clinic*. https://www.mayoclinic.org/healthy-lifestyle/stress-management/in-depth/stress-relief/art-20044456.

McLeod, S. (2015). Freud and the unconscious mind. *Simply Psychology*. https://www.simplypsychology.org/unconscious-mind.html.

Meinzer, K. (2015, 1 April). Surprise! Why the unexpected feels good, and why it's good for us. *The Takeaway*. https://www.wnycstudios.org/podcasts/takeaway/segments/surprise-unexpected-why-it-feels-good-and-why-its-good-us.

Menakem, R. (2017). *My grandmother's hands: Radicalized trauma and the pathway to Mending our Hearts*. Central Recovery Press.

Meshorer, S. (2012, 6 July). What is bliss? *Huffpost Blog*. https://www.huffpost.com.

Miller, G. (2010). How our brains make memories: Surprising new research about the act of remembering may help people with post-traumatic stress disorder. *Smithsonian Magazine*. https://www.smithsonianmag.com/science-nature/how-our-brains-make-memories-14466850/.

National Institute for the Clinical Application of Behavioral Medicine. (2017). [Infographic] *How Trauma Impacts Four Different Types of Memory*. https://www.nicabm.com/trauma-how-trauma-can-impact-4-types-of-memory-infographic/.

Northrup, C. (2018). *Dodging energy vampires: An empath's guide to evading relationships that drain you and restoring your health and power*. Hay House.

Otto, F. (2026, June 13). *Any skill level, making art reduces stress hormones*, Drexel Now. https://drexel.edu/now/archvie/2016/June/art_Hormone_Levels_Lower.

Owen, E. (2021). Collage as a process for reclamation: black collage in conversation with Teri Henderson, New Collection, www.newcollection.com.

Paquette, J. (2015). *Real happiness: Proven paths for contentment, peace & well-being*. PESI Publishing and Media.

Putnam, R. (2019). The symbolism of a triangle: What is the spiritual meaning? *Crystal Clear Intuition*. https://crystalclearintuition.com/symbolism-of-a-triangle/.

Quinn, B. (2019, July 2), Hanna Hoch and collage as protest. *Art History Fashion*. https://www.arthistoryfashion.com/blog/hoch-collage-as-protest.html.

Reed, C. (2019). 10 Reason While Original Art Matters in a Home, Seaside Art Gallery, https://seasideart.com/blogs/blog/10-reasons-why-original-art-matters-in-the-home.

Rozin, P. & Royzman, E. (2001). Negativity bias, negativity dominance, and contagion. *Personality and Social Psychology Review*, 5(4), 296-320.

Smith, J. (2020). *The gratitude project: How the science of thankfulness can rewire our brains for resilience, optimism, and the greater good*. Raincoat Books.

Stutzman, C. (2015, May 17). Keys to stronger relationships. Character Faith Generosity and Leadership, http://chadstutzman.com/?p=1525.

Tippet, K. (2008, February 28). *The inner landscape*. [Interview]. On Being. https://onbeing.org/programs/john-odonohue-the-inner-landscape-of-beauty-aug2017/.

Trippany, R.L., Helm, H. M. & Simpson, L. (2006). Trauma reenactment: Rethinking borderline personality disorder when diagnosing sexual abuse survivors. *Journal of Mental Health Counseling*, 28(2), 95–110.

Wong, D., Baker, C. (1983). Wong & Baker, history of FACES scale, Wong - Baker FACES Foundation.

Zinsmeister, K. (2017, May 5). Giving helps the giver too. *Huffpost*. https://www.huffpost.com/entry/giving-helps-the-giver-to_b_9387064.

ABOUT THE AUTHOR

Laurie Kanyer, MA

Laurie Kanyer, MA, is a retired parent educator, counselor, and organizational consultant. She has worked with individuals, families, and organizations since 1983. Kanyer holds a Master's degree from Saint Mary's University of Minnesota, in Human Development, with a focus on Infant Mental Health, Childhood Grief, and Organizational Development. Kanyer is the author of four books.

She founded Passport to Parenting in association with Yakima Valley Memorial Hospital in 1990, and, as a result, was acknowledged by the United Nations for Inspiring Warmheartedness. The last fifteen years of her career focused specifically on infant mental health, serving pregnant and parenting women experiencing poverty in a program called Growing Capable Parents. This program was in partnership with the State of Washington.

Laurie founded the Yakima Light Project, the first non-profit visual art gallery in the poverty-stricken downtown core of Yakima Washington. In 2015 she was awarded the Washington State Museum Association's Award of Individual Excellence for this project.

Kanyer and her husband Doug have been art collectors since 1978 and most recently founded the Doug+ Laurie Kanyer Art Collection, one of the world's only private art collections focusing exclusively on collage (see Kanyerartcollection.com or @kanyerartcollection on Instagram).

The Kanyers married in 1981 and have three grown children, two sons-in-law and one grandson.

Laurie Kanyer, *Abundance*, 2020, Collage, Doug + Laurie Kanyer Art Collection

ISBN 978-0-578-94261-2

Written by Laurie Kanyer, MA
Co-created by Sarah Best
Edited by Wyatt Kanyer
Junior Design by Jennifer Waldsmith
Senior Design by JuSt Design
Content curated by Lillian Cassidy
Cover art by Michael DeSutter

Library of Congress Publication Data
Names: Kanyer, Laurie MA, Author

Title: *Collage Care: Transforming Your Emotions and Life Experience Using Collage*

Subjects: Psychology, Art, Collage, Personal Transformation, Relationships, Self-Help, Art History

Website: kanyerartcollection.com
Instagram: @kanyerartcollection

Made in the USA
Las Vegas, NV
22 September 2021

30847118R00152